Flourish

LIVE LOVED.
LIVE FEARLESS.
LIVE FREE.

MARGARET FEINBERG

A Note to the Reader:
The paper used to print this book is rated
for pencils and non-bleed inks only.

CONTENTS

Springing with Courage

Growing in Grace

Prepared for Drought

Protected from Floods

Budding with Hope

YOUR INVITATION
TO FLOURISH

I could not have penned a more terrifying personal tale than my previous year. My battle with a life-threatening illness at times stole my will to live. A glut of surgeries altered my body forever. Drugs I can't pronounce fogged my mind and clouded cohesive thought—a serious problem for a writer.

My body ravaged.
My spirit lifeless.
My friendships atrophied.
My connection with God felt frayed.

The Margaret I once knew had slipped away.

Can you empathize? Like me, do you ache for a previous version of life? Perhaps you've been navigating a cavern of deep grief, loss, or loneliness. Years of caring for an ailing parent stripped margin from your life, or raising and releasing your children has prompted questions of purpose and meaning. Pockets of time spent in Scripture or prayer or pews— once sources of happy wonderment—now feel like a chore.

These moments make us feel like the parched soul described by the ancient prophet Jeremiah:

"That person will be like a bush in the wastelands;
    they will not see prosperity when it comes.
They will dwell in the parched places of the desert,
    in a salt land where no one lives."
(Jeremiah 17:5–6)

Are you depressed yet?

You shouldn't be.

Jeremiah refuses to end with this elegy because he knows desolation is not our destination. Instead, the prophet lifts our downcast eyes with hope of revitalization.

"Blessed is the one who trusts in the Lord,
    whose confidence is in him.
They will be like a tree planted by the water
    that sends out its roots by the stream.
It does not fear when heat comes;
    its leaves are always green.
It has no worries in a year of drought
    and never fails to bear fruit."
(Jeremiah 17:7–8)

All who heard Jeremiah's words would have snapped to attention. Ancient Israel sweltered in its arid landscape. An emerald-leafed tree served as a remarkable symbol of life and vitality. The striking image drills deep, but then the prophet adds a detail that's almost absurd: This tree *never* fails to bear fruit.

The metaphor is the modern equivalent of a slot machine that always strikes the jackpot, a lottery ticket dispenser that produces the winning numbers every time, a bank account with unlimited funds.

Eyes open, mouths gape, waves of whispers ripple through the crowd.

Trees in the Bible often serve as metaphors referring to people, not plants.[1] By stacking these two images side-by-side, Jeremiah gives voice to one of life's most weighty decisions. Will we resign ourselves to live like a desert tumbleweed or become a lush and lavish tree? Will we live parched or be planted by a rivulet? Will we wither away or bear clusters of tangy fruit?

Jeremiah presents a choice, but really there is *no* choice.

I'll be the second tree, thank you very much.

The life Jeremiah describes can be summed up in a single word from the Bible: *flourish*.

The word "flourish" pops like corn in the Bible, appearing most often among the poets and the prophets. This agricultural term—*yapriah*, "to blossom" or *parach*, "to bud"—emerges alongside images of trees, grass, vegetation. Sacred excavation reveals layers of meaning within these metaphors.

From the opening biblical command to "be fruitful" (Genesis 1:28), we find God commending behavior that enables creation and humanity to flourish. The text portrays a partnership that leads to both personal and communal flourishing.

Proverbs 14:11 says, "the tent of the upright will flourish," which teaches that a life that flourishes nurtures the community around us. God can "make the dry tree flourish" (Ezekiel 17:24), illustrating that adversity cannot steal God's ability to make us flourish.

Throughout the Psalms, the flourishing of the righteous sings in harmony with peace, a deep sense of shalom. Other passages, such as Psalm 1, show that the virtuous, flourishing life springs from community.[2] This is why I recommend reading this devotional alongside friends.

What does it mean to flourish?

 We flourish when we pursue the life God intends.

When our busy schedules keep us from stopping to love on a hurting friend, we falter. But when we slow to open our arms to embrace the wounded, we flourish.

When we snap back at the difficult coworker, we flop. But if we return the insensitivities with kindness, we flourish.

When our parents' inadequacies make us resentful, we flail. But when we learn to love and honor them despite their imperfections, we flourish.

From Adam and Eve to Abraham and Sarah to Zechariah and Elizabeth, from Genesis to Revelation, flourishing lives serve as signs and symbols of the kingdom of God. God's grace and favor make flourishing possible. Through the Holy Spirit, Christ empowers us to live loved, fearless, and free.

If that isn't enough to make you salivate, here's some whipped cream and a plump, juicy cherry: Our flourishing gives God great satisfaction and joy.

After feeling wilted inside, I committed to unearth what the Bible revealed about a flourishing life. New passages budded with tender blossoms. Old ones burst forth from the winter dormancy and sprang fresh insights.

A handful of traits of the flourishing life emerged…

Planted in Love
    Rooted in Trust
        Grounded in Wisdom
            Nourished by Community
                Springing with Courage
                    Growing in Grace
                        Prepared for Drought
                            Protected from Floods
                                Budding with Hope
                                  Blossoming in Freedom
                                      Ripening with Resilience
                                      Bursting with Life
                                        Cultivated by Christ

Along the way, I harvested a bouquet of surprising scriptural beauties and stories of flourishing I couldn't keep to myself.

I hand them to you as a gift in the hope that we will learn to flourish together.

The lush life awaits.

We can learn to hear God's voice echoing in the everyday.

We can learn to scout for God in the nooks of life.

We can learn to live in awe of God's wonders.

We can learn to burst forth with a joy that cannot be contained.

We can begin flourishing today.

My hope and prayer is that we will learn to thrive alongside our loved ones and sip the sweet nectar of life-giving bonds. To push our roots into the depths of not only the richest, but also the rockiest soil. To tap into the underground river of Living Water.

Blessings,
Margaret

HOW TO USE
THIS DEVOTIONAL

⇢⇢⇢ Fifty-two entries allow you to enjoy this devotional at your own pace. Read one entry per week throughout the year. Or read one each day for eight weeks, then repeat. Do what works best for you. Remember, all is grace.

⇢⇢⇢ For your ease, a box sits next to each entry in the table of contents. Check off the ones you've completed as you read so you don't get lost along the way.

⇢⇢⇢ Each entry concludes with an activity or reflection question and prayer. Take a few moments to dig deeper into what you just read. Even the smallest moments of prayer and silence can be transformative.

⇢⇢⇢ After each month's reading (every four devotions), you'll find a lush coloring page. Grab crayons or colored pencils. Allow your inner creative spirit to flourish. Speak the Scripture aloud. Journal what you discover as you interact with the text.

⇢⇢⇢ Since life is best lived alongside others, *Flourish* is designed to be enjoyed among friends. Invite someone near or far to join you in each of the readings, talk openly about what you're discovering, and pray for each other.

➤➤➤ Share your artwork, your activities, your reflections, your discoveries, your questions through social media. Use hashtag #flourishdevo so we can find each other online and learn to live loved, live fearless, and live free together.

Planted
in
Love

Week 1
THREE WORDS
YOU NEED TO HEAR

Three words exist that you must hear from God today. No matter what your circumstance, this trio of syllables breathes life, imbues hope, infuses joy:

I.

Love.

You.

Lucky for you and me, these three little words emerge again and again throughout Scripture. Each page reveals the bigheartedness of God and his endless reservoirs of love.

"I paid a huge price for you… That's how much you mean to me! That's how much I love you! I'd sell off the whole world to get you back, trade the creation just for you" (Isaiah 43:4 MSG).

That's just one seedling from the Old Testament.

In the New Testament, Jesus talks about love, teaches about love, models love. He even sacrifices his body because he loves you so much.

Why does God use the entire Bible and thousands of years of history to talk about love?

Because he wants us to flourish and knows that can only happen when we hear and believe those three words.

Maybe like me, you are all too aware of your faults and failures, your shortcoming and slipups. While we may never ask someone, "Am I loveable?" we spend oodles of time wondering.

I confess that sometimes I modify my behavior to satisfy their silent cravings. I orchestrate an adorable outfit so I can receive more compliments. Or I try to win someone's affection by purchasing them an outrageously generous gift. If the person responds with affirmation or accolade, I pretend it's nothing at all. Yet deep down, I wish they'd say more. Perhaps their words would dull the ache that accompanies my suspicion that I'm not lovable.

Perhaps you do that, too.

Yet God alone provides satisfying responses to our deepest doubts, our most mangled fears. Through the spyglass of Scripture, we see the abundant love of God isn't just some abstract theological idea, but a gift that is real and that we can experience every day.

 Jesus empowers us to move from recognizing God's love to receiving God's love.

Recently, I confessed to God that I felt unlovable. As I aired my feelings, I reflected on his expressions of love in the Scripture. When I arrived at Psalm 33:5: "The earth is full of his unfailing love," my eyes grew damp. The response swelled like sea surf before crashing over my soul.

God's fierce love is abounding, bounteous, crammed, bursting, jammed full, running over, teeming, overflowing, never in short supply. Divine affection orbits and permeates and saturates. God's love never ends. Tears plopped on the page.

The emotional reaction left me puzzled. I'm not a teary person and go to great lengths to avoid becoming misty—including avoiding all Nicholas Sparks movies.

By then I was weeping.

When I regained my composure, I realized Scripture exposed my hidden questions, doubts, and angst regarding God's love. I believe in my cranium he loves me but strain to receive his affection in the fibers of my being.

On far too many days, God's love doesn't feel palpable or perceptible. Though I proclaim God's love to others, such divine affection often feels like it's for someone else, anyone else, just not me. Yet the passages reveal God's love as closer, more faithful, more bountiful than I comprehend in the nooks and crannies of every day.

Life's difficulties, disappointments, and flat out disasters often twist our perspectives of our core identities. They convince us we do not belong, we do not matter, that our lives are inconsequential. The coarseness of life can close us off from absorbing and receiving God's good gifts.

Like a plant seeks water, punching through packed soil, splitting solid rock, in some cases moving mountains to drink from an underground spring, we are created to thirst and discover the fullness of life found in God and his love.

After I finished reflecting on Scripture and dried my eyes, a prayer emanated from my lips:

God, open me to the fullness of your love. Awaken me to your divine affection.

I wondered why I hadn't done this sooner. Love is the foundation for faith and knowing God, yet I'd never set apart specific time to marinate in the truth of God's fierce love. I ended my time hopeful—and yes, even happier.

FLOURISH TODAY: Turn to page 27 and color Jeremiah 31:3, inserting your name into the promise: "I have loved you, _____, with an everlasting love." Snap a photo and share with your friends online using #flourishdevo

THIS WEEK'S PRAYER: *Father, Open me to the fullness of your love. Awaken me to your divine affection. Amen.*

Week 2
THE NATURE OF LOVE

How do you recharge your emotional and physical batteries? Some people frolic in the ocean. Others prefer stillness and solitude. Others draw energy from celebrating with a crowd of friends. For me, the wonders of a hike in the mountains rejuvenate my core.

Maybe that's one of the reasons I find Jesus' teachings magnetic. He loves to instruct from nature, about nature, with nature. He preaches from stony mountaintops, wheat fields, even the middle of a lake. Farmers and foxes and hens take leading roles in stories. He handpicks fisherman as disciples and nicknames himself the Good Shepherd. Divulging his nature through nature, he orders the squalls and sea spray obey him.

What does Jesus' affection for creation have to do with love?

Much.

In one of Jesus' most famous sermons, he speaks of creation to unearth a crucial dimension of love.

"Look at the birds of the air," Jesus counsels in Matthew 6:26, followed by, "See how the flowers of the field grow" (v. 28).

Jesus says those who follow him are to become birders and botanists, people who fix their eyes on ravens and lilies, specimens that display the good, the lovely, the admirable. But this command is more than an invitation to join the Sierra Club.

If we're living in white-hot pursuit of God, Jesus says, the focus of our lives will shift. Everyday details like what's missing from the brunch menu to the ever-changing fashion boots trends will lose their importance. We will become less fussy and more grateful.

Jesus insists on this refocusing. Life tends to draw our gaze downward in discouragement and inward in selfishness. But Jesus tells us to squint outward and upward. We must branch out to admire the robins, canaries, and hummingbirds and listen to them whisper rumors of another world.

Their physical presence reminds us of the invisible God who holds together all things. Though we may be tempted to question or doubt God's loving-kindness, these feathery friends display God's unbridled love for his creatures.

"Look at the birds of the air; they do not sow or reap or store away in barns, and yet your heavenly Father feeds them. *Are you not much more valuable than they?*" (Matthew 6:26)

There's more. Because Jesus' encouragement to focus on nature is lassoed to a lesson about why it matters.

"See how the flowers of the field grow... If that is how God clothes the grass of the field, which is here today and tomorrow is thrown into the fire, *will he not much more clothe you—you of little faith?*" (vv. 28–30).

Jesus' teachings beat back the propaganda that we don't matter to God. That we must strain forward on our own. That the weight rests on our spines. That we master our own destinies.

In this pen of hogwash, Jesus turns our eyes to the featured creatures and asks, "Are you not worth much more than they?"

Jesus highlights our incalculable worth. Our preciousness cannot be weighed in carats. As God's prized possession, we do not have to live our lives grasping for that which is freely given.

Being planted in love means perceiving our immeasurable value to God.

 **You may not think you matter to God,
but you matter more to God than you think.**

The first century Jews to whom Jesus preached should have known this truth already. The Old Testament speaks of God as jealous and possessive, and the ancient writers meant this in the best possible way.

God's people are referred to as God's possession. The repetition of "I am your God" and "You are mine" echoes from the Bible in the laws, the decrees, the commands, the calls to holiness.[3]

God's love for you can be seen in nature because if he created masterpieces like a tangerine sunset or a crimson rose, imagine how much more artistry he accomplished when he created you.

When you're tempted to believe you aren't worthy of God's love, take a hike. Literally. Rush outdoors and observe God's handiwork. Look over here and there and everywhere. Eye the furry and the feathery. Observe the vivid, velvety, and wooly creations.

Consider the careful craftsmanship behind fashioning one breath, one wing, one petal. Reflect on the loving care the Maker takes in every creative expression. They are beautiful, but they pale in comparison to you.

That's how much God loves you.

FLOURISH TODAY: Step out your front door. Identify three things in creation that God values. Pause. Breathe deep. Now reflect on how much more God loves you. Repeat, if necessary.

THIS WEEK'S PRAYER: *Father, When I feel unworthy, help me to notice the reminders of your love all around me. Amen.*

Week 3

CONFESSIONS OF
A RECOVERING PERFECTIONIST

Hello, my name is Margaret Feinberg, and I am a recovering perfectionist.

I like my life and my house and my workspace to be tidy and clean and in proper order. When I fail, I beat myself up. When I succeed, I don't take time to rest or celebrate before moving on to the next task.

Perfectionism ranks among the worst flaws because of its natural positive feedback mechanism. A perfectionist lives frustrated by flaws, and since perfectionism is a flaw, perfectionists exist in a constant state of frustration.

Even if you're not a perfectionist, you can still become discouraged by your flaws. Perhaps that's why Jesus' roster of disciples provides great comfort. One might expect Jesus to handpick the best and brightest. Would you expect any less from the Son of God?

Plus, tick-tock, Jesus only has thirty-six months of ministry. He can't afford to take unnecessary risks if he hopes to accomplish his mission in such a short span of time.

But, as it turns out, Jesus would have made a lousy kickball captain. He doesn't select the strongest, most agile players. He skips over the smarty pants valedictorians and Ivy League graduates. Instead, Jesus assembles an improbable team.

Luke 6:13 records: "When morning came, he called his disciples to him and chose twelve of them, whom he also designated apostles."

Peter—impetuous, brazen, competitive, waffler

Andrew—lives in the shadow of his brother, Peter

James—a son of "thunder," edging for the front row

John—a son of "thunder," full of hot air and swagger

Philip—limited by his experience

Bartholomew—lacks a filter

Matthew—shady past as a tax collector

Thomas—must I remind you of his colossal doubt?

Simon the Zealot—freedom fighter

Jude—way too quiet, not likely to be selected for class president

Judas—a greedy backstabber

What's-his-name?—that obscure guy no one can remember

A list like this makes the perfectionist in me as nervous as an introvert at a housewarming party.

Jesus takes an enormous risk. His every act endures heavy scrutiny. Religious paparazzi tail Jesus snapping mental images of his movements, his comebacks, his companions. The trackers share their discoveries with the religious hierarchy. They spend hours dissecting every syllable, every interaction.

Luke 6:7 says, "The Pharisees and the teachers of the law were looking for a reason to accuse Jesus." The religious powerbrokers work around the clock to snare the Son of God, so he can't afford a roster of liabilities.

The religious leaders nitpick Jesus. By contrast, Jesus' screening process for his disciples elevates the lowly. He reminds us that the kingdom of God doesn't expand through the work of religious paparazzi and spiritual overachievers. God isn't limited by our imperfections.

God fiercely loves us through our flaws and imperfections—not in spite of them.

Sometimes I count my flaws as reasons to be disqualified by God. Maybe you do, too. I've never been the keenest in any class, the swiftest in any sport, the most agile in any activity.

As a senior in high school, I took the SAT for college admission. I scored a 410 in English. I think you receive a score of 400 for writing your name at the top of the page. Yet despite the absence of a large vocabulary and creating far too many nonwords (according to my husband, Leif), I've published dozens of books and Bible studies.

Our weaknesses and flaws can become portals for God's grace, windows to display his glory. When imperfect people trust God and do their best to follow him, they become glimmers of goodness, and we can only assume that something or Someone else must be at work.

Jesus' selection of the disciples reveals that God's affection for us never wavers—whether we score big or run up a deficit on life's ledger.

 **When we're at our very worst,
God still loves us as if we're at our very best.**

No matter how you feel about yourself or your life today, Jesus invites you to find your way back home to the open arms of the Father. To be enfolded in his warm embrace. To bask in his joyous grin over you.

Whenever your flaws overwhelm you, think of the flawed followers of Jesus who are revered as apostles. He loves you just as dearly as he loved them and offers you the privilege of serving him. Just as you are.

Live loved amid your many flaws. You're in good company.

FLOURISH TODAY: Identify three specifics you don't like about yourself. Thank God for the imperfections and the opportunity they provide to display God's grace and his glory.

THIS WEEK'S PRAYER: *Father, Thank you for loving flawed disciples like me. Amen.*

Week 4
LIVE LOVE AND GIVE LOVE

Love's short four-letter construction is deceiving. The word seems so simple: L-O-V-E. But trying to understand love can leave your head spinning. *What does that four-letter word look like? How does it work? And why does love seem so difficult to conjure up when it comes to that nasty next door neighbor?*

Adventurous by nature, I converted my questions into a spiritual caper. I scoured the Bible from front to back, from *alef* to *tav*, to log teachings about love. From this, I developed a catalog of the characteristics of love. If I knew how to identify love, I could spot it among counterfeits.

A curious pattern soon emerged: Love moves. While I imagined love like a colossal ruby-red heart that sat stationary, love wiggles and squirms more than a sugar-filled toddler.

Love rejoices.
Love protects.
Love trusts.
Love forgives.
Love hopes.
Love perseveres.
Love leads.
Love keeps.
Love abounds.

More than a string of letters, a word can change based on its function. My elementary English teacher called this the "part of speech." Though I often think of love steady as a noun, love glides like a verb. Much like a liquid, love splashes and splatters, infiltrates and infuses, careens and cascades. The imagery stirred my longing to dive into the subterranean depths of God's love.

The more Scripture I explored, the more I believed and received God's love. Then I smacked into 1 John 4:19–21: "We love [God] because he first loved us . . . Anyone who loves God must also love their brother and sister."

Gulp.

 Love finds a way to you then through you.

Because of its verby nature, love cannot become dammed up with us. The L-word floods into our lives, nourishes our spirits, then animates our actions. We *fill* with love and then we *spill* with love. When we drench others with love, God refills and overflows our holding tanks.

I prayed to become more attuned to the needs of others. The changes were slow like the way dripping water reshapes a stone.

An elderly woman needed a place to sit. I gave her mine.

A father of two at the checkout seemed rushed. I offered him my place in line.

The lady next to me in the waiting room wanted to chat. I put down my magazine and enjoyed her company.

People appeared before me that I hadn't seen before, or rather, hadn't wanted to see before. Living loved nudged me to engage, to embrace, to serve each one—even in the slightest of ways. More than anything, I desired that these people lived loved, too. Overflowing with God's affection, I longed for as many people as possible to join the party and discover how beautifully loved they are.

This transformational process didn't come without a struggle. I argued uncharitably with the customer service guy of my cell phone carrier. I snipped at a sales clerk for her slow service. Leif returned home late from work to find me critical instead of compassionate.

If you try to give the love you've received from God, expect moments of wincing and strain. Love that is shared with you must be spread to others.

When you flounder and fail to dispense, don't give in to defeat. Instead, seize the opportunity to recommit yourself to living loved and giving love.

The way of love rumbles and tumbles, a mysterious path fraught with failure and frustration. When you're tempted to throw up your hands and yell, "I can't," listen for the still voice of God to whisper:

"No, *you* can't. But *my love* can."

FLOURISH TODAY: Think back to a time when someone made you feel most loved. Duplicate that action in the life of someone who needs it today.

THIS WEEK'S PRAYER: *Father, Help me to make more room for your love in my life by pouring it out to others. Amen.*

Pray & Reflect

I have
loved you, _____ ,
with an
everlasting love.
With
unfailing love
I have drawn you to myself.

JEREMIAH 31:3 NIV

Rooted in Trust

Week 5
A CASTING CALL

No one knows what waits around the next bend. Our health and our jobs and our friendships don't include guarantees. Eliminating uncertainty from our lives remains impossible. The moment uncertainty vanishes in one area of life ambiguity reappears in another like a game of a Whack-a-Mole.

I know this all too well from my work.

Many people equate self-employment with freedom. Images emerge of making your own schedule, commanding your own ship. Whatever you say goes. No one outranks you.

After working among the self-employed for years, I've discovered these as myths. Though you may not have a single person to call "boss," life soon constricts with forces like deadlines, invoices, employees, taxes, and contracts. Working for yourself can feel like being a long-tailed cat in a room full of rockers.

The self-employed are forced to live in a house haunted by uncertainty.

Where will I derive income two years from now? I don't know. What will I do in the case of disability? I don't know. Who will provide for our employees if the economy plunges? I don't know. What will I do if my aging parents' health fails and they need my assistance?

I.

Don't.

Know.

Those are scary words and staring them down turns your knees into Jell-O pudding pops.

As we wither under the weight of uncertainty, Jesus speaks this truth:

"So do not worry, saying, 'What shall we eat?' or 'What shall we drink?' or 'What shall we wear?' For the pagans run after all these things, and your heavenly Father knows that you need them. But seek first his kingdom and his righteousness, and all these things will be given to you as well. Therefore do not worry about tomorrow, for tomorrow will worry about itself. Each day has enough trouble of its own" (Matthew 6: 31–34).

Even if life serves you a plate of uncertainty, Jesus says, you don't have to order a side of worry. You can live fearless.

Your fears about tomorrow can be confronted today. God knows what you need *today*, and God works to meet those needs *today*. Don't let tomorrow's uncertainty rob you of today's joy.

All easier said than done. Rooting yourself in trust amid the swirl of uncertainties sounds simple. But how do we burrow into deeper trust in God?

"Cast your cares on the LORD and he will sustain you" (Psalm 55:22).

Trust requires action and doesn't develop on its own. Trusting requires casting, and casting means communicating and handing our cares over to God.

Casting our cares on God frees because it gives feet to our trust.

What do you fear about the future? What unknown circumstance haunts you at night? Have you shared this with God?

Uncertainty makes us feel like a child left alone in the dark while playing hide-and-seek. We stay still and quiet, hoping to remain invisible, unnoticed.

One of my biggest uncertainties comes in the area of finances. We've been through many seasons when I didn't know if we'd have enough income to pay our employees. The fear of scarcity rummages through my soul revealing how little I trust God.

When I consider the last five years, God provided every time. I remember one particular stretch where I crunched all the numbers, and the math revealed we'd live without paychecks for many months. Somehow, and I still can't explain it, God provided and sustained.

But if you observed my worry during that time, you'd think God was a baker who hadn't provided a crumb in years.

The core issue has never been money, but trust. More funding would never alleviate the anxiety in my heart.

I'm learning to break the silence and bring my uncertainties to God and then trust him to carry them for me. Rather than bury them in the recesses my heart, I must exhume and hand them to the only one with the power to manage them.

Whatever the source of your unease, know that Jesus wants to handle your fears about tomorrow today.

Cast your cares on him, share your deepest fears, and you'll soon discover:

 The crux of uncertainty is the very place God wants to meet you.

FLOURISH TODAY: Memorize Psalm 55:22: "Cast your cares on the LORD and he will sustain you." When you feel the pangs of uncertainty recite it in your mind.

THIS WEEK'S PRAYER: *Father, Thank you for providing for today's needs and handling tomorrow's uncertainties. Amen.*

Week 6
HOW TO GROW IN TRUST

One of the most profound characters in the Bible never makes an appearance on the pages of Scripture yet offers a model of trust. Sound confusing? Let me explain.

Luke 7 mentions a centurion with an ill servant. The centurion treasures this worker and sends the Jewish elders to plead with Jesus to make a house call to heal this servant.

Here's the breakdown in the ancient Roman military:

A chiliarch commands 1000 soldiers.
A centurion commands 100 soldiers.
A decurion commands 10 soldiers.

In modern terms, the centurion ranks as middle management. Don't let the title dupe you—he's an A-list leader. This savvy Gentile sends Jewish messengers to Jesus who respected the centurion enough that they work overtime convincing Jesus. They speak of the man's heavy investment in their lives and place of worship.

Jesus travels to the centurion's address.

"[Jesus] was not far from the house when the centurion sent friends to say to him: 'Lord, don't trouble yourself, for I do not deserve to have you come under my roof. That is why I did not even consider myself worthy to come to you. But say the word, and my servant will be healed" (Luke 7:6–7).

The man displays an astounding trust in Christ—so much so that this is one of the few times Jesus is described as being "amazed." Jesus even says that this Gentile's faith ranks greater than that of any Jew in Israel.

What impresses Jesus?

The centurion's trust that Jesus could heal his son through declaration.

The authority of Christ is not bound by space. The power of Jesus' word transcends miles and kilometers, inches and centimeters. Unlike any other healer, Jesus doesn't require physical presence or a magical incantation.

When the messengers return to the centurion's house, they discover the servant's health flourishing.

Though this Roman leader never appears in the pages of Scripture, his words and actions become a rich example of what it means to be rooted in trust.

Not only is the centurion humble ("I do not deserve") but he is also faithful ("But say the word"). These two characteristics combine like hydrogen and oxygen to create a wellspring of trust.

Trust requires being humble enough to realize you can't solve your problems. Only God can. Trust requires being faithful enough to believe God is willing to work on your behalf and proactive enough to ask him to intervene.

If you struggle with trust as I do, this story might discourage you.

What if I don't have enough trust to "amaze" Jesus? I wonder. *Will he not be able to work in my life?*

What should we do when our faith feels more like a speck of mustard dust instead of a mustard seed? We must remember:

 God remains faithful even when we are faithless.

Some days we march in unshakable confidence like the centurion. Others we meander in doubt.

Yet Christ invites us to lean into his authority and trust. The one who controls the winds and waves has power over your situation and circumstances.

God holds all things together including you.

On my most doubt-filled days, I find it helpful to confess my feelings of powerlessness to God. I ask God to fill with me the faith I do not have. To awaken a childlike trust in him.

Then I practice a simple exercise. I center my mind on Jesus, and begin a breath prayer: I breathe in the goodness of God— "You are good"— and exhale the faithfulness of God—"You are faithful." My breath becomes a petition that God will reveal the depths of his goodness and faithfulness in my life.

The practice of this breath prayer often transforms into a time of natural adoration of God. Somewhere along the way, infused with his grace, my resolve to trust grows stronger. And I remember that God can do much even with a speck of mustard dust.

FLOURISH TODAY: What situation are you struggling to trust God with? Pray a bold, centurion prayer to reassert your confidence in God.

THIS WEEK'S PRAYER: *Father, I do not deserve your grace, but I trust that you are able to work for my good and your glory. Amen.*

Week 7

WHEN YOU FEEL
GOD LET YOU DOWN

Years ago, I joined a fledgling church community that longed for God to bring revival. We prayed for God to renew and expand this church and bring spiritual awakening to the community. Many members experienced dreams and visions of the coming growth and transformation.

Days rolled into weeks and months and years. Attendance flatlined. Still no revival.

Then the news broke: The pastor had an affair. People migrated elsewhere. The church deteriorated. Many of us felt disillusioned and disappointed.

Why hadn't God come through for us?

Those waiting on the Messiah asked a similar question. For centuries religious leaders prayed and watched and expected the emergence of the long-awaited king of Israel. A military conqueror. An emancipator. The anointed one to restore Israel to its proper place.

Enter a carpenter's son. No fanfare or pomp and circumstance. Just a baby born in a trough to an unwed momma.

After Jesus' baptism in the Jordan, people are even more baffled by Joseph's son. Those who have yearning for the arrival of the Messiah don't always recognize Jesus.

Disillusioned.

Disappointed.

Confused.

Perhaps that's what those in Jerusalem sensed soon after this Jewish man enters the city gates on the back of a donkey.

Picture it: Strangers rip palm branches from low limbs, creating a walkway of fresh scented foliage. More than a red carpet, the people of Jerusalem roll out a mishmashed quilt of love. Scarves overlap with tunics, coats crisscross with wraps. Songs burst with expectation.

"Hosanna," they cry in Matthew 21:9.

The word means "praise God" or "save now." Jesus enters the city as their Savior. The wide-eyed and wonderstruck crowds rejoice at the arrival of the long awaited One.

But Jesus doesn't deliver what they expect. Instead of taking his seat on the throne, he is nailed to a cross. Rather than spend time with the religious elite, he hangs out with ragamuffins.

Those who shout, "Hosanna" are drowned out by those who now scream, "Crucify him!"[4]

Two thousand years into the future, we may be tempted to judge the crowd for the fickleness of their hearts. But how quickly do *we* dart from shouting blessings to God to sweeping him under the rug?

We too can:

turn on a dime,

trade teams,

abandon our savior,

forsake the one who has fed us,

waver in trust.

I can't read this passage without wincing. Because I, too, am among the fickle of heart. One day I shout of God's faithfulness; the next I wonder why he deserted me.

If you've ever felt disappointed by God, maybe you do, too.

Perhaps you've felt the sting of the spouse who cheated or the kids who never visit or the friend who betrayed you. Whatever the experience, God didn't live up to your expectations, and trusting him doesn't feel safe.

The crowd sentenced their savior to death, but let's not forget how the story ends. The crucified one soon rises from the dead. Many realize that Jesus never let them down. The resurrection reveals much including:

 God hasn't given up on you even if you have given up on him.

Your heavenly Father wants to help you move from fickle to faithful, from skeptical to trusting.

Perhaps God rode into your life bursting with promise and you have crucified him for not meeting your expectations. Now is the time to ask him to be resurrected in your life and return to the throne of trust where he belongs.

FLOURISH TODAY: Get real and don't hold back. Confess your disappointments *with* God *to* God.

THIS WEEK'S PRAYER: *Father, Resurrect your presence in my life and restore my trust in you. Amen.*

Week 8
NOT THE ONLY ONE
IN THE DETAILS

Ask any of my friends and they will tell you that I have more than my fair share of crazypants ideas. A few years ago, I hatched a doozy. I invited friends online to join me in reading the Bible in forty days for Lent. The *whole* Bible.

66 books.
1,189 chapters.
31,102 verses.
All in 40 days.

The project was not without frustrations and failures.

Some days I fell far behind.
Some days my eyes glazed over.
Some days I wondered, "What did I just read?"
Some days I thought, "*That* story is in the Bible?!"
Some days my spirit awoke to vivid imagery, poetic words, and haunting stories.

Along the way, the books of the Bible I most dreaded became my favorites.

For example, I assumed things like root canals, scrubbing a sewer, and scooping up after my dog, Hershey, sounded more delightful than reading the book of Numbers. As the namesake suggests, this fourth book of the Torah packs a numerical punch, and I'm a wordsmith, not an accountant.

The reading failed to connect at first. The addition and subtraction appeared tedious. *Who cares about the results of an ancient census?* Nevertheless, I slogged through the roll calls and begets and tribes and generations, and amidst the piles of data God whispered: *"See, I care about the details."*

When it comes to trusting God, I'm accustomed to handing over the big projects. Hanging stars. Spinning planets. Raising and lowering the sun. My faith doesn't buckle with colossal feats.

But among smaller acts, I have a nasty habit of inserting myself into the action. Giving God a hand up. Taking control of the situation. Becoming upset about minute details.

I am beginning to discover:

God reveals himself in the details.
God speaks through the details.
God loves us in the details.

Some people say "the devil is in the details," but God is there, too. When we're wading through life's minutiae, we must learn to relinquish the teensy weensy to him, too. The pile of bills. Patience with the kiddos. The crazy neighbor. Waiting for the perfect housing situation to open up. Finding a new friend. These may seem small and inconsequential to the creator of the universe, but:

God can be trusted in *all* things— the mammoth and microscopic, the teensy and tremendous.

Learning to trust God more deeply empowers us to view every event as an opportunity to grow in trust. Dallas Willard challenges us to search high and low for the "the *competence* and *faithfulness* of God."[5]

I believe God is faithful, but I often second-guess his competency. That's why I thrust myself in the middle of situations where I don't belong. Open my mouth when I should bite my tongue. Snatch the steering wheel when I should be content riding shotgun.

With this realization, I began praying a simple prayer: *God, show yourself as competent and faithful.*

This potent prayer forced me to search for God in the details. To note the competency of God in situations where I hadn't considered his presence:

The unexpected, last-minute houseguest that throws me into a tizzy because every room is a mess.

The morning appointment than runs long and ruins my plans for the rest of the day.

Through this prayer, the everyday interruptions became intersections for God to redirect my steps and best-laid plans. Instead of annoyances, I began seeing these as divine interludes, living more wide-eyed for the people I'd encounter, the "Only God" moments he had in store.

On a deeper level, the prayer pried open my death grip on control and expanded my heart to truth. *Show yourself as competent*, I prayed, into a fractured friendship, a flubbed communication, a dead car battery, the news of a friend's suicide.

And indeed, God did. I became awestruck by the renewal of a friendship, the gift of a difficult but rewarding conversation, the kindness of a mechanic, the comfort of a community.

God turned out to be working in the mondo and miniscule—I could trust him as much with my vehicle and my soul as with the stars.

I double dare you to pray a similar prayer: *God, show yourself as competent and faithful in my life.* With each God-encounter, your roots of trust will grow deeper, and you'll live every day just a little more fearless.

FLOURISH TODAY: Grab a Mason jar and write, "God's Got This" on the side. Place a slab of sticky notes nearby. Whenever God reveals his competence and faithfulness, write down the moment on a note and drop in the jar. You'll be surprised just how fast the jar fills up.

THIS WEEK'S PRAYER: *Father, show yourself as competent and faithful. Amen.*

Pray & Reflect

Cast your cares on the LORD and he will sustain you.

PSALM 55:22

Grounded
in
Wisdom

Week 9

DRAW FROM
THE RIGHT SOURCE

Has someone ever said something to you that cut you to your core and left you feeling like a bloody heap on a polished floor?

A few years ago, I finished speaking at a leadership conference when a man approached me with a rather blunt question: "What gives you the right, as a woman, to get up and speak to this audience, which includes men, and talk regarding anything having to do with Scripture?"

I froze.

What the man did not know was that, in the months leading up to this encounter, I had been asking God for greater wisdom. I scouted Scripture for wisdom's every appearance. I soaked up wisdom from older and more seasoned Christ-followers in my life.

Before I could cognitively process my response to the man's question, the words tumbled of my mouth: "Because I am God's daughter."

I felt like I had delivered a candle into a room of gunpowder. But the man looked at me, recognizing the principle that a daughter—whether on behalf of a heavenly father or a human one—has a right to speak on behalf of the family.

"That's a good answer," he replied.

As I reflect on the simple response, I recognize the words carried a depth which was neither defensive nor offensive. I could have given many answers, both theological and theoretical, but the simplicity of wisdom rested on my lips.

God heard my prayers and provided the perfect packet of wisdom in the moment.

Learning to live in wisdom is an artful undertaking whereby Christ embeds himself in us so that wisdom may become part of us. In this divine equation, the more I spend in Christ's presence—through prayer, worship, Scripture—the more I grow in his wisdom, the more I share his wisdom.

 Soaking in divine wisdom leads to sharing God's vision.

As I search for wisdom in my daily life, I find that it often displays itself in the simplest of answers and the most concise of responses. Wisdom asks just the right questions to expose falsehood or cuts to the core issue others attempt to skirt.

But never mistake wit for wisdom.

We can easily confuse wisdom for pat answers, platitudes and empty one-liners. If you don't know what I mean, just check the memes on your Instagram feed and the overused quotes on your friend's Pinterest board. Sometimes the most "like"-ables obscure the complexity of the matter to which they're addressed, just as a quote out of context can be used to misinterpret the very truth it was written to lift up.

The source of all wisdom is God, and wisdom promotes open-eyed obedience to God. Wisdom herself—as personified in the Hebrew—invites us to go deeper in our friendship with God and underscores the value of personal and communal well-being. This way of life dignifies and enhances the flourishing of others.

"For *the Lord* gives wisdom; from *his* mouth come knowledge and understanding. *He* holds success in store for the upright, he is a shield to those whose walk is blameless," (Proverbs 2:6–7).

Perhaps one of the deepest wells of wisdom ever drawn is the book of Proverbs. The book is primarily written under the auspices of King David's son, Solomon, whom the Bible describes as the wisest man ever to have lived.

Proverbs does not just provide a selection of pithy maxims. This is more than an ancient Facebook wall. These potent chapters help us develop a deep moral sensibility—both personally and communally—that's founded on the Source of all wisdom. This book teaches that revering the Lord is the beginning of wisdom, and you become what you revere.

Proverbs ground us in the life God intends.

Want to build a life with the things money can't buy? Deepen your trust in God: "Those who trust in their riches will fall, but the righteous will thrive like a green leaf" (Proverbs 11:28).

Want to establish a life filled with integrity? Embrace honesty in every facet of your life: "The house of the wicked will be destroyed, but the tent of the upright will flourish" (Proverbs 14:11).

The wisdom of God will challenge your short-term and long-term decisions. It will help you make the best possible decisions for yourself and your community.

Want to find wisdom? She is calling from the pages of Proverbs, inviting you to share in the feast of life laid out on her table—life as God intends, a rich, full, flourishing life.[6]

FLOURISH TODAY: Each day this month, read one chapter of Proverbs. The 31 chapters are a custom-made fit for most months.

THIS WEEK'S PRAYER: *Father, Ground my life in your rich wisdom. Amen.*

Week 10

THE BEST FRIEND
YOU'LL EVER HAVE

I'd like to introduce you to the most remarkable woman in the Bible. She's the most vibrant, life-giving, breathtaking female ever mentioned in Scripture, ever seen in history. She holds more wealth than the world's richest business tycoon and more power than the world's savviest politician.

If you make her your companion, you'll discover the best friend you've ever known. She will encourage you. She will counsel you. She will protect you. She will strengthen you. She's got your back. But if you get on her bad side, cross her, or snub her, she will become your fiercest enemy.

Her name is Wisdom.

The writers of Proverbs personify wisdom as a lovely lady. This poetic language uses rich metaphors to create a vivid image of just how much we need her in our life.

Wisdom is vital for all life's big questions: *What should I do in this phase of life? Should I purchase the house? Should I accept the job offer? How do I hold my marriage together? How do I parent my adult child well? Where will I find the time and money to care for my aging parents?*

 When questions elude you and answers escape you, wisdom is gifted to guide you.

Befriending wisdom is the wisest thing you can do.

"Blessed are those who find wisdom,
    those who gain understanding,
for she is more profitable than silver
    and yields better returns than gold.
She is more precious than rubies;
    nothing you desire can compare with her.
Long life is in her right hand;
    in her left hand are riches and honor.
Her ways are pleasant ways,
    and all her paths are peace." (Proverbs 3:13–17)

With irony, Proverbs teaches that laying hold of wisdom requires wisdom. In other words, wisdom is the key to unlocking the proverbs.

What do you need to know to ground yourself in wisdom as you dive into the book of Proverbs?

The proverbs not only direct you to make good decisions; they guide you to make godly decisions. That's why when you read this book of wisdom you must move at a leisurely and contemplative pace. The goal is not to work through the proverbs but to allow the proverbs to work through you.

Proverbs provide practical, portable truth, but we should not mistake proverbs for guarantees from God. These aphorisms speak to the general way life works.

Consider Proverbs 10:4: "Lazy hands make for poverty, but diligent hands bring wealth."

As a general principle, hard working people discover success. But what happens if a hardworking person becomes chronically ill or a slacker wins the Powerball?

We must receive proverbs for the truth they encapsulate, not as a permanent pledge of how life will turn out.

We are meant to marinate in wisdom until it becomes part of the way we think and respond—until wisdom saturates every fiber of our being.

The wisdom found in its pages don't just protect us, they protect everyone else, too. As Proverbs 29:2 encourages, "When the righteous flourish, the people rejoice" (HCSB).

The principles taught don't just help us experience the joy of being God's people and flourishes through our life, they are designed to empower communities to prosper.

Perhaps that's one reason why Proverbs, along with the rest of the Bible, are best read in community. Why? Because you can isolate a proverb from the rest of Scripture and find justification for a self-centered life. This ancient book warns that a proverb in the mouth of a fool is as "limp as a wet noodle" and "like putting a scalpel in the hands of a drunk" (Proverbs 26:7, 9 MSG).

Friends don't let friends misread Proverbs.

The beauty of Wisdom is that she speaks to anyone who will listen and befriends everyone who welcomes her companionship.

Proverbs 1:20–21 describes, "Out in the open wisdom calls aloud, she raises her voice in the public square; on top of the wall she cries out, at the city gate she makes her speech."

Wisdom stands in the public square clamoring for the attention of any passerby. Her message isn't directed to the ruling class, wealthy or elite, but anyone and everyone—including you and me.[7]

FLOURISH TODAY: With prayer, consider the wisest, Jesus-follower you know. Set up a lunch and spend time asking questions and gaining godly wisdom.

THIS WEEK'S PRAYER: *Father, Remind me today that a drop of your wisdom is better than an ocean of earthly knowledge. Amen.*

Week 11

WHEN ONLY FOOLS RUSH IN

"You can do better. You're not going to wear it."

Carolyn's words were the last I wanted to hear. Our shopping expedition had already taken us to a dozen stores.

I slipped on the pale blue peasant dress with intricate stitching around the collar. The fit felt boxy and the color washed me out, but the 60 percent off sticker was calling my name. I didn't want to return home empty-handed, so I made the purchase anyway.

Exiting the store, a rush of endorphins pulsated through me. The shoppers high lasted all afternoon.

I meant to wear the dress that weekend, but reached for an outfit with a more flattering fit and complementary color. The next week I had a wedding, but the dress didn't seem, well, dressy enough. Over time, the purchase migrated toward the back of my closet.

Six months later, I pulled out the garment, tags still dangling, and tossed it into a donation bag.

My shopping buddy had tried to advise me of what I knew but refused to hear.

"The way of fools seems right to them, but the wise listen to advice" (Proverbs 12:15).

Solomon talks about fools almost two dozen times in Proverbs and Ecclesiastes.

The term refers to a hardheaded person who thinks they don't need anyone else's advice, a thickheaded person who sticks their fingers in their ears whenever others speak wisdom, a narrow-minded person who thinks they have a monopoly on the best answers.

I'd never applied the word "fool" to myself, but if I couldn't accept the advice of a trusted friend in a simple, everyday decision, I wondered where else I might be responding more like a fool than a wise person?

Who else had attempted to offer good counsel in my work, my relationships, my spiritual growth, my life, and I had become dismissive or defensive?

In *Necessary Endings*, Dr. Henry Cloud summarizes how the styles of behavior for wise and foolish people differ.

Wise people are ready learners who are eager to listen to feedback, make adjustments, and grow.

Foolish people play the blame game and in the process become defensive, refuse to take ownership, and resist making a change or taking advice.[8]

The primary difference between a wise person and a fool rests in how a person receives instruction and correction. I'd love to say this is the only time I resisted wise advice, but sometimes I'm overly eager to dismiss a suggestion or counter with why the idea just won't work.

The temptation to dismiss wise counsel pulls strong.

Perhaps this is what King Solomon alludes to when he writes: "As a dog returns to his own vomit, so a fool repeats his folly" (Proverbs 26:11 NKJV).

We must resist the temptation.

If the wise man's eyes fill with light, the fool stumbles in darkness.

If the wise man sees and investigates, the fool tumbles into danger unaware.

If the wise man takes time to listen, the fool rushes to answer.

If the wise man walks in knowledge and understanding, the fool struts in deceit.

Fools scoff and brush off wisdom.

 To flourish in the life God intends, we must be grounded in wisdom and root out foolishness.

How do we know when we're playing the fool? Check the following that are true for you. We recognize foolish behaviors in ourselves when we:

_____ live defensively (Proverbs 9:7–8).

_____ attract attention to ourselves (Proverbs 9:13).

_____ badmouth others (Proverbs 10:18).

_____ flare with annoyance (Proverbs 12:16).

_____ disregard sound advice (Proverbs 12:15).

_____ are quick to quarrel (Proverbs 20:3).

_____ need to be always right (Proverbs 26:12).

It's always easier to recognize these tendencies in others than ourselves. Yet how often do we let these foolish behaviors slip into our own lives? These proverbs serve as guardrails to keep us on the path of wisdom.

One of the ways I've been working on rooting out foolish behaviors is by giving permission to people who know me and love me to help recognize foolishness in my actions, behavior, or words. Sometimes it's hard to hear, but with patience, prayer, and tenacity, I'm beginning to recognize and correct my behaviors.

To flourish, you must be grounded in wisdom. This means rooting out the foolishness no matter how big the sale may be.

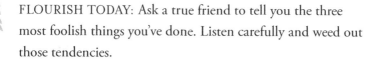

FLOURISH TODAY: Ask a true friend to tell you the three most foolish things you've done. Listen carefully and weed out those tendencies.

THIS WEEK'S PRAYER: *Father, Help me weed out the folly in my life and ground myself in your wisdom. Amen.*

Week 12
EARS, HEART, AND HANDS

"Hear, O Israel: the LORD our God, the LORD is one" (Deuteronomy 6:4).

These words, known to Jews as the opening of the Shema, were central to Jesus' prayer life.

For thousands of years, Jews have recited the Shema, a collection of passages from the opening books of the Bible. The three portions of Scripture that make up the Shema include Deuteronomy 6:4–9, Deuteronomy 11:13–21, and Numbers 15:37–41. This trinity of passages serves as an ongoing reminder to the Jewish people of their commitment to God.

Jesus likely learned the Shema as a boy. So it is not surprising that Jesus quoted from the Shema on at least one occasion:

"Hear, O Israel: The Lord our God, the Lord is one" (Mark 12:29).

Jesus goes on from this reference, drawn from Deuteronomy to speak of loving God and loving each other. But by starting where he does, Jesus teaches us a valuable lesson:

 Learning to love is learning to listen.

Hear, O Israel.

Perhaps Jesus knew how the command—Hear, O Israel—could fall on deaf ears, not just the Israelites, but ours, as endless voices vie for our attention. Amidst the brouhaha of busyness and rowdy demands, the clamor becomes deafening. We are unable hear to the still, gentle voice of God in our lives.

How often has your spouse or parent or child or friend said something like, "Heeeeelllllllloooo. Are you listening to me?" You snap back from whatever your mind was drifted, smile, nod, and pretend that you heard every word. When they ask you to repeat what they said, your face turns crimson.

What they covet in that moment is not just attention, but affection. They want you to show them that they are a priority to you. To place what they are relaying to you above your to-do list and text messages and tax returns.

In essence, when someone makes a bid for your attention, they are ask, "Do you love me?"

We see that our ears are connected to our head. What is not so obvious is their connection to our heart.

This principle applies to our earthly *and* heavenly friendships. If you love God, you'll listen to God. You'll seek God through prayer and Scripture and your ears will fill your heart again and again with God's word and your life will be more grounded with divine wisdom.

But there's even more to Jesus' words.

Hear, O Israel.

In Hebrew, the command to "hear" is the word *shema*. This suggests more than auditory intake or perceiving a sound.

Shema encompasses the ideas of attentiveness, taking heed, and responding with action.[9]

When the psalmist cries, "LORD, hear my prayer" (Psalm 143:1), the songwriter isn't saying that God needs a hearing aid. He's calling on God to take action, to respond—to answer his prayers.

Our ears must connect to our heads, our hearts, and our hands.

In the life of faith, a gulf exists between hearing and doing. We attend church on Sunday, but by Wednesday afternoon forget what we learned. We read a passage in the Bible, and the truth bounces off our forehead instead of burning into our heart. We receive a clear nudge from God to serve then sit on our hands.

The wisdom we receive is only as good as our willingness to act on it.

Jesus tells a tale of two men who complete construction on new homes in Luke 6:46-49. One builds on a slab and one on silt. A category five hurricane makes landfall. The homeowner who engineers on the slab loses a few shutters. The one whose foundational frame rests on silt loses everything.

The story illustrates the difference between auditory versus action based responses. The two men had their choice of silt or solid rock but one wasn't wise. Even though both heard the same teachings, only one practiced *shema*. Jesus teaches that the foundation of our faith rests on obedience.

If you love God, you must listen to God. When you listen to God, he will speak wisdom in your life. The next part is up to you. Will you obey or not?

Heavy rains are inevitable, so ground yourself in wisdom.

FLOURISH TODAY: What is God asking you to do right now? Do it before the sun sets tonight.

THIS WEEK'S PRAYER: *Father, Give me the courage to act on your divine wisdom. Amen.*

Pray & Reflect

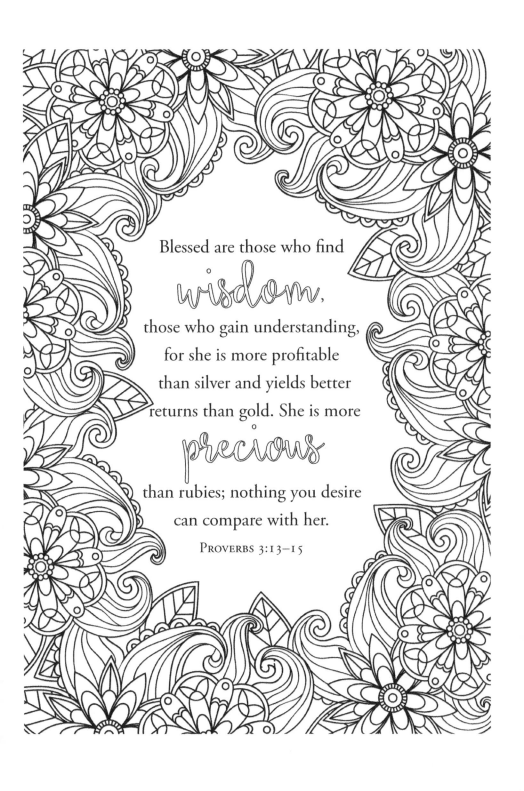

Blessed are those who find

wisdom,

those who gain understanding,
for she is more profitable
than silver and yields better
returns than gold. She is more

precious

than rubies; nothing you desire
can compare with her.

Proverbs 3:13–15

Nourished
by
Community

Week 13

THE POWER OF PAIRS

From Florida to North Carolina to Colorado to Alaska to Colorado again and now to Utah. Nothing teaches the value of friendships like boxing up your life and moving hundreds of miles away.

As a person who craves adventure, part of me enjoys starting over. A rush of adrenaline. The fireworks of change. The challenge of a new launch.

But moving takes a brutal toll. Boxes. Tape. Dinged tables. Shattered lamps. Items pulled from the back of closets that stir forgotten memories—some beautiful, others broken.

Which box did we pack the colander in again?

When the thrill wears off, I feel unsettled and discombobulated, lost and lonely.

For the first few months in Utah I felt like I was holding my breath. I sipped oxygen but never exhaled.

Do you know what that feels like?

Scared of the unfamiliar.
Flustered by the uncertainty.
Uprooted from the life you knew.

Moving to a new state means losing my people.

Friendships, like oxygen, allow me to breathe in the fullness of life.

I'm not alone. Studies show that the quantity and quality of our social connection—including friendships, family bonds, closeness of neighbors, and warmth toward strangers—form a direct link to our personal happiness and well-being. The connection is so tight they're almost inseparable. *We cannot flourish alone.*

We soon met people in Utah, but the budding bonds couldn't replace the friendships I nurtured in Colorado for decades.

Years of friendship expand like rings of a tree. Not only can you count them but they speak of the storms weathered, flash floods survived, long warm summers relished.

Every ring, every year, a gift.

Maybe that's why moving feels so uprooting.

Jesus reminds us of the importance of community when he chooses a dozen followers-turned-friends to journey with him in ministry. He reiterates this point when he commissions those disciples to embark on their own ministries.

"Now after this the Lord appointed seventy others, and sent them in *pairs* ahead of Him to every city and place where He Himself was going to come" (Luke 10:1 NASB).

Jesus appoints seventy, then he pulls a Noah. He sends them out two by two.

Why?

Perhaps because he knows our effectiveness increases when we're grafted together. If one wavers, the other digs in roots. When one feels fragile, another stands sturdy.

Spiritual leaders from Scripture receive encouragement in the form of friends, followers, and besties. Shiprah and Puah, Moses and Aaron, David and Jonathan, Naomi and Ruth—just to name a few.

This truth of ministry runs parallel to a truth of life. Living free does not mean living alone. We must surround ourselves with people who are for us and love us

for companionship,

for celebration,

for long days,

for dark nights,

for encouragement,

for hard conversations,

for rich community.

Building these friendships takes time, intentionality, and physical presence. Some friendships naturally run deeper than others.

Again, that's okay. Learning to laugh and cry and console and serve well together happens ever so gradual. To know and be known is never a quick process.

Having moved many times throughout my life, I've learned that it takes two or more years to develop deep-rooted friendships in a new place. Those friendships often go through a series of developmental stages.

The first stage is getting to know each others' likes and dislikes as acquaintances. We may see each other at church or grab a cup of coffee.

Stage two involves discovering each others' stories in depth and risking vulnerability. This often involves longer activities together like meals or workouts or tackling a shared project.

Stage three involves conflict and disagreement which is always dicey. But if we can learn to communicate and honor differing perspectives, the relationship deepens.

Over time, the relationship may enter stage four which I call *friendimacy*. This is hanging out in your jammies, without makeup, sharing the deepest levels of hopes, dreams, fears about God and life with each other.

Not every person will become a stage-four friend, and that's okay. Some friends will settle into the first three stages, but when you find *friendimacy*, I believe you should hold onto it for life.

A few verses after he commissions his disciples in pairs, Jesus instructs them to travel extra light—without a money belt, extra bags, or shoes.

73

Pair stands in stark contrast to everything Jesus then tells them leave behind. Jesus reveals that the items they consider necessities aren't as crucial as each other.

Go without anything, but whatever you do, don't go it alone. In order to pursue the life God intends, we need *pairs*.

We may not flourish *within* a particular community, but we will never flourish *without* community.

When we're intentional about relationships with other believers—investing, loving, risking vulnerability—something wondiferous happens. Jesus joins the party.

Community nourishes us...

no matter how many times we move,
no matter how many times we transition,
no matter how many times we are sent out.

When we find community, we discover Jesus, too.

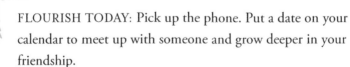

FLOURISH TODAY: Pick up the phone. Put a date on your calendar to meet up with someone and grow deeper in your friendship.

THIS WEEK'S PRAYER: *Father, Reveal the people you want me to do life with. Amen.*

MORE THAN A MEAL

When you come for dinner at our house, be forewarned that we don't eat at the dining room table. We prefer the living room, feet propped on the stained, barn-wood coffee table. Our superpup, Hershey, snoozing on the fluffy, white rug nearby.

This disarms new friends; meals grow intimate and cozy.

If you had a time machine and travelled back 100 years, meals would function quite differently. You'd find formal dining tables with ample place-settings that formed a barrier around each diner: bread plates and knives at nine o'clock, water glass at one, champagne flute at two. Three forks to the left of the plate and a knife and two spoons to the right, all lined up on an imaginary baseline. This created a well-drawn semi-circle of personal space.

For Leif and me, this sounds like purgatory.

Of course, we comply with decorum on special occasions and attempt to follow rules of fine dining establishments. But when we're with friends, we prefer gathering around our rustic living room table, because we believe relaxed, extended meals bring people together.

In ancient Israel, an invitation to share a meal was an invitation to share a life. Dining together served as an act of establishing intimacy, of experiencing life together. In antiquity, you ate with people who shared your values and thus were your friends or whom you wanted to share your values and thus become your friends.

Consider Jesus' words in Revelation 3:20: "Behold, I stand at the door and knock; if anyone hears My voice and opens the door, I will come in to him and will dine with him, and he with Me" (NASB).

When we grant Jesus access, he makes himself at home in our lives. He pulls up a stool to our kitchen counter, a chair at the dining table, a cozy spot on the couch ready to feast with us. To share the first course of a life-long banquet of love and truth and grace.

We ask God to sustain us with his life, to take up residence within us through the body and blood of his son. Jesus approaches us with the intent of intimate friendship. If we allow him in, he will dine with us, and together we'll start the Jesus-life, eating from his plate, dipping in his dish, discovering him as the source of our nourishment.

Why are tables and feasting so central to the biblical concept of community?

Because meals bind us together. We dish stories from our lives across the table, pile on seconds, and lick our forks before dessert. When we join together around a common table we experience intimacy—both in our homes and the table Christ prepares for us. In essence, we are saying, "Here we are, all eaters and drinkers. This is what makes us human."

 Around the table, we discover a gathering place for the home and a feast for the heart.

Meals fill up bellies and break down barriers.

When we stop, sit, and eat with others, we set aside

inequality,

loneliness,

busyness.

At mealtime, we share our most human needs in the company of others who hunger and thirst the same.

At least, that's what we *should* do. Often we refuse to share our hearts, much less our food. Or we build fortress walls, perhaps unspoken and invisible, around the topics that make us uncomfortable. Our fears barricade us from double dipping into each others' lives.

How can you make your mealtimes an intentional invitation to share life?

My friend, Kathryn, recently invited nine people, most who didn't know each other, for dinner. She turned down the lights, lit a few candles, set out the fabric napkins.

I watched as she masterfully transformed dinner into a profound time of connection. She slowed the meal by serving salad first, followed by roasted vegetables and grilled pork.

The portions were small. Rather than offer seconds, she pulled out an array of deserts ranging from fresh cut pineapple and strawberries to a lemon cake. She set out a cheese platter with grapes.

"Eat slow," she encouraged. "This is designed for lingering together."

We stayed late into the night forging new friendships and solidifying old ones. With warm mugs of coffee in hand, the conversation ebbed and flowed, and as we neared midnight we realized time had passed faster than any of us had realized. Somewhere along the way something special happened: We felt like we had experienced the deepness of Christ-centered conversation and bonds.

What barriers have you erected around your table that keeps others from knowing and being known? Break the rules you've accepted and open your heart as wide as your mouth.

FLOURISH TODAY: Invite a friend you want to know better into your home, and share a simple homemade meal. Eat. Talk. Laugh. Connect. Perhaps ditch the dining room and cozy up on the couch instead.

THIS WEEK'S PRAYER: *Father, Grace the table in my home with your presence so I can know others and be more fully known. Amen.*

Week 15
FLOCKING TOGETHER

Not many people will meet a real-life shepherd in their lifetimes, but there I stood in a muddy Oregon field alongside Lynne and her flock. She spoke of the animals she adored, reminding me of the importance of gathering with other believers.

Watching these wooly creatures graze, she explained that sheep are defenseless. They are naturally timid. Flocking together becomes their primary defense. That's why whenever a predator approaches, flocks gather close. This is their only protection.

"What happens to the sheep that wanders off on its own?" I asked Lynne.

Lynne explained that wanderers are picked off by predators or infected by parasites. Some overindulge in grass until they become ill. Only under the watchful eye of a good shepherd can a flock of sheep enjoy a healthy, flourishing life.

After God creates Adam, some of his first words are, "It is not good for the man to be alone" (Genesis 2:18). God created community to nourish us, sustain us, protect us.

Jesus calls twelve followers who form a band of spiritual brothers as one of his first acts of ministry. In the Acts account of Pentecost, the Holy Spirit descends on the people gathered together.

But we aren't just built for *any* community; we are meant to be part of the church. We are made to gather with those who follow the Good Shepherd.

After Jesus ascends into heaven and the beautiful chaos of Pentecost fades, what do the Jesus-followers do? As Acts 2:42–47 records, they continue gathering together and being nourished as a community.

They teach the story of God.
They spend time together.
They share meals.
They harmonize.
They petition and praise.

The love they share for their Good Shepherd binds them together in one flock. Reflecting on these passages, I'm always intrigued by how little the Bible shares of the logistics of what they do when they're together. We observe sacred melodies, holy encouragement, spiritual training, and sharing meals, but what about the format? The length? The location? The order? The time of day?

_If_ we gather with other believers matters more than _how_ we gather.

Our sinful nature, petty grievances, and selfish desires expose themselves in the company of fellow Jesus-followers, not so that we become divided and bitter, but so that we may live free, redeemed, and created into all God has called and created us to be.

The church lays the formative foundation where we learn to live out the ministry of reconciliation (2 Corinthians 5:18). Community becomes ground zero of learning to live loved, live fearless, and live free.

As members of God's flock, we have the opportunity to mature together and learn how to function properly with our unique gifts, talents, and callings.

Along the way, we garner strength for our own faith journeys and we may even find that the gathering of Christians, the church, and this adventure of following Jesus are not only fun—but contagious.

Our love and unity become an invitation for the world to know Jesus. May we be a people who live as the beautiful bride of Christ.

FLOURISH TODAY: If you don't have a church, visit one this week. If you're currently church surfing, pick one. If you're part of a church, look for a new area where you can serve, study, or become more involved.

THIS WEEK'S PRAYER: *Father, Help me to love the church as much as you do. Amen.*

Week 16
WHEN CHURCH BRUISES

Trying to find a church to attend feels like trying to buy a new pair of shoes. The options and fit and styles don't make the decision easier.

One Sunday morning, I struck up a conversation with a smartly dressed thirty-something woman at a church Leif and I were visiting. She invited me to her house for a small group gathering.

I bounded like a schoolgirl in pigtails on the brink of breaking into the cool kid crowd. I'd finally be able to connect with others my age, grow in my faith, and learn fun details about our city. I counted down the days until the gathering.

Sporting a new blouse and made-from-scratch chocolate chip cookies, I felt giddy as I pressed the doorbell. More than a dozen women gathered around for a scrumptious meal. The conversation moved naturally, unforced. Afterward, we relocated to the living room where one woman shared her story. She told intimate details of her painful past and disclosed the depression and fear of mental illness she'd wrestled with her entire life.

The room sat silent. More than anything, I wanted to wrap my arms around her and whisper how much she was loved, laud her bravery, and remind her that Christ was with her in the midst—and we would be, too.

As a newcomer, I knew to wait for the leader's response.

"Why haven't you been more honest about this before?" she retorted.

I felt stunned, as if I'd been knocked on the head by a platform pump. This precious woman, who just exposed some of the most hidden parts of her soul, sat with tears running down her face. The moment pleaded for compassion, the comfort of Scripture, and much prayer. Instead, a spate of brutal cross-examination questions confronted her.

I kept waiting for someone to turn to the ancient truths of Scripture or offer a prayer on her behalf. When no such comfort was offered, I spoke up and reminded the woman of the tender freedom and healing available in Christ. The leader shot me an icy stare, as if I'd said something wrong.

The junior therapy questions continued until the leader abruptly changed the conversation to find out if everyone was ready for s'mores. I grabbed a slab of dark chocolate and slipped out the front door. On the drive home, I struggled to wrap my mind around what I'd witnessed—someone hurting so much and no one offering any comfort or even a prayer.

I resolved to continue attending the small group. Maybe I could be that voice. Perhaps I could win their trust and begin working prayer and some sort of Bible reading into the small group. But I received an email notifying me that I wasn't welcome back. The group decided that they didn't want to make room for any new members, and that meant me.

I wept. For two days.

Maybe you've been hurt by an encounter in church, too. Someone in the church harmed you, or a leader of the church let you down. The community you expected to nourish you, instead, left you depleted.

Being in a church isn't easy for many people—including me. The church, by nature, is flawed, broken, inefficient, dysfunctional. Despite these weaknesses, God has chosen to stamp his name on her.

Paul writes in Ephesians 5:25, "Husbands, love your wives, as Christ loved the church and gave himself up for her."

 The church may have frizzy hair, smeared makeup, and holes in her dress, but she is still the bride of Christ.

Knowing Christ cherishes her and desires her as his own makes me want to love her, defend her, and serve her.

The church is where the poor have their needs met by the rich, and the rich discover that they need the poor. Where the heavily burdened find willing backs to share the load. Where the restorers speak louder than the destroyers. Where an orphan discovers a family, and a wanderer finds a home. Where all are welcome, the seekers and explorers right alongside the finders and guiders.

In this place called church, I rediscover that I am not alone on this journey of following Christ. I'm reminded that I only have a snapshot of the panoramic story of what God is doing in this generation and the grander story of what he has been doing throughout history.

Amid its flaws, the two-thousand-year-old church stands as a constant reminder that God has not failed us yet. Nor will he ever.

FLOURISH TODAY: Do something outrageously kind and generous for someone in the church who has hurt you.

THIS WEEK'S PRAYER: *Father, Help to heal the hurts the church has caused in me and learn to love her again. Amen.*

Pray & Reflect

Now after this
the Lord appointed

seventy others,

and sent them in pairs
ahead of Him to every
city and place where He
Himself was going to come.

LUKE 10:1 NASB

Springing
with
Courage

DARE TO DRAW NEAR

A recent study showed that children's play is more free and creative when they remain within a close radius of their parents. Within this circle of affection and affirmation, the children are willing to take risks, try new activities, and stand up again after falling down. The study found that the presence of a person who loved them unconditionally made all the difference.[10]

This physical design of earthly children reflects on the spiritual design of our heavenly Father.

Our proximity to God is crucial to beating back anxiety and living fearless.

The Bible provides countless ways to draw near to God and experience his presence in our lives. Holy Communion. Worship. Silence. Solitude. Community. Service. Spiritual friendship. Prayer. And many more.

For me, when I begin the morning by marinating in God's Word, I find myself living loved and living with less fear. The day sparkles brighter as the Scripture prepares me to extend unsuspecting kindness, become more willing to take risks. Anchoring myself in the love of God frees me to spring with courage and extend that love in daring ways.

When I don't refresh myself with the presence of God—due to busyness or laziness—anxiety steals my resolve.

The moment I return to his presence, divine affection and affirmation saturate me with a sense of security and safety. Within close radius to God's presence, I can live a more open-handed life ready to embrace others.

Obeying the Bible's command to fight anxiety requires more than extracting something from our lives. We need a fresh infusion of the presence of God to flourish.

You can dare to be brave when you remain within a tight radius around God. The reality of staying close to God twinkles amid Paul's prescription:

"Do not be anxious about anything, but in every situation, by prayer and petition, with thanksgiving, present your requests to God. And the peace of God, which transcends all understanding, will guard your hearts and your minds in Christ Jesus" (Philippians 4:6–7).

Notice that Paul doesn't prescribe avoiding the severity of the situation. Nor does he instruct us to attempt to modify our behavior on our own. He doesn't provide a hyperlink to a podcast from a motivational speaker or offer an easy six-step process with a downloadable infographic.

Instead, he places his hands on our shoulders and walks us back to the loving presence of our heavenly parent.

Alas, if I am honest, all too often I turn to God as a last resort to solving my anxieties and fears. Common first steps might include downward spirals, angry outbursts, slipping into a funk. One of my most common coping mechanisms for anxiety is food.

Sweet potato fries, anyone?

My doctor says that our adrenal glands can become overworked
and stop functioning properly when we live in a constant state of anxiety.
This leaves our bodies fatigued and tempts us to turn to sugar, caffeine,
and carbohydrates for energy and a mood boost.

But Paul says that rather than put something in our mouths, we should
let something out of them—prayer and thanksgiving. These simple
ingredients cannot be found on most people's recipe for courage,
but Paul lists them as essentials.

Praying over our anxieties by name helps us surrender them to
God. Thanking God for what he has already done, and like Israel,
remembering the mighty acts of God become a launching pad for
trusting God more deeply.

As we recall his faithfulness of the past, we are more prone to trust in
the present. When I'm most tempted to doubt if God will get me
through a current difficulty—whether financial pressures, a broken
relationship, or ongoing physical ailment—I pull out a sheet of paper
and create a list of all the times God carried me through in the past.
The list becomes a living testament of God's goodness and faithfulness
that infuses me with courage to move forward.

In addition to remembrance, prayer and thanksgiving become the
one-two punch in the battle against worry. As we follow Jesus deeper
into God's presence, anxiety lessens. Fears fade in the background.

Worry goes by the wayside, and we spring with courage. We are more confident in our ability to step out and be brave while in proximity of our creator.

 Every fear issues an invitation to draw near.

This is what the apostle Paul nudges us toward when he instructs us to not be anxious in *anything*, but respond to *every* tough time with prayer and gratitude to God. As we reorient ourselves Godward, we rediscover his presence, his perspective, his peace.

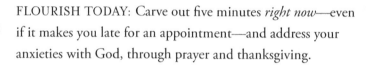

FLOURISH TODAY: Carve out five minutes *right now*—even if it makes you late for an appointment—and address your anxieties with God, through prayer and thanksgiving.

THIS WEEK'S PRAYER: *Father, Thank you for transforming my deepest anxieties into holy courage for the sake of your kingdom. Amen.*

Week 18
REFLECT ON THE NAME

One night I awoke to the sound of someone in the kitchen rustling through papers. I tried to reach over to wake Leif but my arm refused to move. I gulped for breath. My eyes scanning the ceiling. I lay paralyzed in terror.

"Leif," I whispered.

Nothing.

I whispered louder.

My arm regained its strength. I shook Leif's shoulder.

"Do you hear that?" I asked.

Our eyes locked. He reached under the bed where he kept an extra long, metal flashlight that doubled as a baton.

He crept toward the bedroom door. The hinge creaked. The light switch snapped on.

"What is it?" I asked in a hushed voice.

"Come see," Leif chuckled.

A beady-eyed mouse had been wreaking havoc in our kitchen.

Whether it's the slam of shutters, crackle of thunder, or rustling of a mouse, sounds that disrupt my sleep leave me rattled.

Now I don't usually respond to the same sounds during the day. Something about the nature of darkness and the inability to see magnifies my fear. I'm not afraid of the dark itself but what's in the darkness, what's in the unknown, what's in the uncertainty.

When I was a little girl my parents taught me the power of the name of Jesus. Sometimes when I awoke from bone-chilling night terrors, I said Jesus' name again and again until I felt peace.

"Therefore God exalted him to the highest place and gave him the name that is above every name, that at the name of Jesus every knee should bow, in heaven and on earth and under the earth" (Philippians 2:9–10).

The name of Jesus is greater than every other name. Jesus' name carries power and authority.

Throughout the Bible, a person's name often reveals much about a person's character. They are like keyholes to understand the nature and attributes of God as well as provide us with truths that can fortify our faith during moments of fear.

When you find yourself sinking in anxiety or worry, saying God's name out loud can comfort you, empower you, renew your courage. By knowing and reflecting on the names of God, we can move from focusing on the fear to fixing our eyes on the Father.

I've found courage arising when I speak the name of God that fits the specific fear that I'm facing.

Perhaps you're struggling to land a job, facing financial worries, or even bankruptcy.

Jehovah-jireh means "the Lord who provides."

Or you feel lost, alone, forgotten.

Jehovah-raah means "the Lord my shepherd."

Maybe you're facing a difficult diagnosis, the breakdown of your body, or a health crisis.

Jehovah-rophe means "the Lord who heals."

Maybe you're feeling like life is out of control, and you're tempted to give up.

El-Shaddai means "God Almighty."

Or you're struggling with healing from your past or facing a temptation.

Jehovah-m'kaddesh means "the God who sanctifies."

Maybe you're feeling overwhelmed and crippled by fear.

Jehovah-nissi means "God our banner."

Or you're in the middle of a spiritual battle where you're struggling to make progress.

Jehovah-nissi means "the Lord who reigns victorious."

Maybe you're feeling weakened and worn out.

Elohim means "strong One" or "God"

Perhaps you struggle to identify the root of your anxiety and fear.

Jehovah-shalom means: "the Lord of peace."

Or you feel trapped and without hope.

Jehovah-shammah means "the Lord is present."

Each name reveals a facet of the character of God and helps us understand more of his power, might, and wonder. Studying the names of God grounds us in the truth of who God is and how he moves in our lives.

We all face fears, but we do not have to fear them alone.

 The names of God remind us that wherever we go, God is already there.

He provides, leads, and strengthens. He infuses us with fresh peace and hope.

The next time you're overcome with fear, reflect on the names of our great God. Your fears begin to shrink to the size of our kitchen-raiding mouse. No matter how big our crisis, he is bigger still.

FLOURISH TODAY: Commit three names of God to memory. Reflect on the way God has revealed these facets of his character to you in the past and promises to in the future.

THIS WEEK'S PRAYER: *Father, Help me to trust who you are in my life so fear doesn't reign anymore. Amen.*

Week 19

MENDING A DIVIDED MIND

The details remain fuzzy but I still experience flashbacks of approaching a mall escalator as a girl. Perhaps I was unruly or my shoelace was untied. I only remember the warning of the adult who accompanied me, "If you don't stand still on the center the of the escalator stair, a trap door will open and you'll be eaten by crocodiles."

The threat of dinosaur-age reptiles felt real to this Florida native. From that moment on, I worried every time I stepped on moving stairs. It wasn't until I was a teenager that I realized every mall doesn't store crocodiles under their escalators. Only that one.

To this day, I'm extra careful each time I step on an escalator.

The oldest of five children, Dave remembers that whenever his family went to a restaurant and the children became loud, his father resorted to the ominous fear tactic of announcing, "The man is coming!"

Dave grew up terrified police officers were coming to arrest him for his behavior. Years later he still shrinks back whenever he hears a siren or sees law enforcement.

My friend Molly shared that as a young girl she was instructed to take the elevator to meet her mom on an upper floor. She pushed the wrong button and ended up lost. More than twenty years later she doesn't like elevators. If given the choice, she always takes the stairs.

Janie had a strange uncle who squeezed ketchup and mustard on her feet when she was a young girl and would chase her around, catch her and then nibble on her feet. "He was weird," she says. "But to this day I can't stand anyone touching my feet."

Fears and worries from childhood can haunt us for decades.

The origin of the word "worry" when it first appeared in Old English meant, "to strangle." Over the centuries, it transitioned to mean "to bite and shake" much like a dog treats a rubber toy. In the early nineteenth century, worry adopted a more modern meaning of being persistently anxious.

Most of us develop unconscious movements in response to our worries. We spot the habits in others before we see them in ourselves. Tense muscles, tapping fingers, bouncing knees, curling toes, pacing in circles, cracking knuckles, and playing with hair may indicate the presence of worry.

Jesus fuses a command with a query regarding our concerns, "Do not worry about your life... Which of you by worrying can add a single hour to his life's span?" (Luke 12:22, 25 NASB).

Jesus begins with instructions so simple that it almost trivializes our feelings. Perhaps Jesus knows that, in some sense, even our most serious worries are miniscule in comparison to God's ability to solve them or use them for our good.

Then, Jesus uses a rhetorical question to remind us of what we already know: Worry accomplishes nothing.

How many of life problems have you solved from stewing and worrying?

 Worry weakens your resolve without resolving your weakness.

Instead of solving our problems, worry intensifies our problems by fracturing our minds and diverting our thinking.

The Greek word for worry, *merimnao*, stems from two words:

merizo (divide)

nous (mind)

Worry splits our focus between tomorrow and today leaving us exhausted. No wonder the apostle James describes a double-minded person as unstable (James 1:8). No one makes good decisions when they are anxious.

I know because I struggle with worry—and not just when standing on an escalator. I'm most prone to worry anytime after 9:00 p.m.

The worry gremlins come for me after nightfall when my body is worn, my resolve wobbly, my self-control weakened.

Sometimes I toss and turn until I'm strangled by sheets tied up in a Pandora's box of irrational anxieties. In broad daylight, the issues would appear manageable, but darkness casts ghastly shadows.

On more nights that I want to admit, I lay wide awake, staring at the ceiling fan, my mind spinning over an issue. Part of me says trust God

101

and stop allowing worry to pickpocket my much-needed sleep. The other part spends hours replaying every scenario until I craft a back-up plan to the back-up plan.

Jesus instructs us to confront our worries by exposing their silliness.

Can worrying about this matter buy me groceries or pay the rent or send me on vacation? Will stewing over this solve the problem? Is God bigger than this concern and able to handle this in a way that is good and reveals himself as competent?

You already know the answers to these questions. And God already sees the path through your most worrisome situations.

FLOURISH TODAY: Make a list of your most irrational fears. Confront them by asking questions that expose their silliness.

THIS WEEK'S PRAYER: *Father, Mend my divided and worrisome mind so that I am more focused on you. Amen.*

Week 20

HOLY CHUTZPAH

The highest compliment my Jewish grandmother ever handed out to me: "She's got chutzpah!" (pronounced *hoot-spuh*).

Perhaps because my Jewish grandmother didn't dispense many compliments. (You need a Jewish grandmother to know why that's funny).

In my Jewish father's home, chutzpah was a good thing, meaning you had courage, strength, bravery, a willingness to say or do whatever it took. The Yiddish term describes someone with nerve or bravado expressed in an inspiring way. Sometimes chutzpah is defined as "shameless audacity" or "impudence."

That's why, a few years ago, I started posting a "Morning Chutzpah" on Twitter; a quote from a thinker, writer, entertainer that's got some POW and BLAM to it.

After the launch of Morning Chutzpah, people asked, "What's chutzpah?"

I thought everyone had a Jewish grandmother. *Oi veh.*

Sometimes the quotes are reflective. Or ironic. Or zany. Or funny. All contain chutzpah.

Scripture records an account where Jesus rewards a Canaanite woman's chutzpah: "Lord, son of David, have mercy on me! My daughter is demon-possessed and suffering terribly!" (Matthew 15:22).

Jesus initially ignores the woman. After being brushed off like a crumb from the table, she bats away social norms and expectations. With a high-pitch shrill, she pleads for Christ's pity. Will Jesus heal her daughter? She refuses to leave without an answer.

The woman stomps on everyone's last nerve, twice—especially the disciples, who urge their Rabbi, "Send her away, for she keeps crying out after us" (v. 23).

One word zaps from the page: keeps.

This miniature, unassuming syllable explodes with holy chutzpah.

She keeps...

> Chasing
>> Hounding
>>> Urging
>>>> Trusting
>>>>> Zeroing in
>>>>>> Pleading
>>>>>>> Asking
>>>>>>>> Hoping.

This living, breathing portrait of holy chutzpah refuses to quit.

Again, Jesus brushes her off reminding her that he came only for the lost sheep of Israel. As a Canaanite, she doesn't make the cut.

The tenacious woman refuses to relinquish. She throws her torso at his feet: "Lord, help me!" (v. 25).

Again, Jesus dismisses her. Only those with bad manners dispense the food of the children to the dogs, he says. The mulish woman, again, refuses to let go: "Even the dogs eat the crumbs that fall from their master's table!" (v. 27).

Then the whole story stands on its head.

"Woman you have great faith!" Jesus says. "Your request is granted" (v. 28).

The woman's holy chutzpah reveals a precious insight: God values persistence, insistence, and dogged determination.

Springing with courage means more than overcoming fear, worry, and anxiety. It requires determination and persistence in the face of obstacles.

Have you lost that sparky fight? Is your get-up-and-go gauge reading "empty"? Have you stopped asking God for big things, including your healing?

 Persistent, consistent prayers stabilize wobbly, weary faith.

A few years ago, I was diagnosed with cancer. Through the brutal fight—which included chemotherapy, radiation, and many surgeries—I prayed for zero. A prayer for zero means zero cancer cells, zero side effects, zero complications, zero allergic reactions. But I *keep* praying for zero. I still ask God that every cancer cell in my body be eliminated.

Maybe you need the courage to pray for zero, too. For zero sleepless nights, zero financial burdens, zero negative reactions, zero conflicts at work, zero bullies at school.

My resolve was restored by the dogged determination of the Canaanite woman. My hope is that yours will be, too.

Awaken holy tenacity. Embrace holy chutzpah. Pursue God until he gives you an answer. And don't let go.

FLOURISH TODAY: What is one bold or outlandish prayer you've lost resolve to pray? Write it down, post it in a place you see often, and begin asking for it every single day this week, starting today.

THIS WEEK'S PRAYER: *Father, Give me courage to be persistent and pray bold prayers. Amen.*

Pray & Reflect

Do not be anxious about *anything*, but in every situation, by prayer and petition, with thanksgiving, present your requests to God. And the peace of God, which transcends all understanding, will guard your hearts and your minds in Christ Jesus.

PHILIPPIANS 4:6–7

Growing in Grace

Week 21

THE WARRANTY
OF EVERYDAY GRACE

The used-car salesman assured me I had nothing to worry about. The vehicle we were purchasing only burned diesel fuel, and I was nervous that in an absentminded moment, I might opt for gasoline.

"It's physically impossible to make that error," the salesman promised. "The unleaded nozzle simply won't fit into a diesel tank."

We took the salesman at his word and zoomed around town in our new-to-us vehicle for more than a year.

But one day, after filling up at a gas station, I heard a metallic noise from the front of the car while driving. *They need to do some roadwork,* I reasoned. The clanging and clattering grew brasher.

There's no way. I couldn't. I didn't. I . . . oh no.

My stomach sank as I realized the fuel nozzle slipped in without friction. I had just filled Leif's diesel car with unleaded.

I withdrew my foot from the accelerator and pulled to the side of the road. I confessed my mistake to Leif on the phone, and he called a tow truck.

That night I lay awake tossing in sweaty sheets, spinning in regret. I prayed some crazy prayers: *Please let there be no damage. Please let this be no big deal. Jesus, just as you turned water into wine, will you turn unleaded into diesel—puh-leez.*

The dealership called early the next morning to inform me that I'd done around $7000 worth of damage.

I struggled to catch my breath.

"But I have some good news for you," the mechanic said. "The warranty will cover it."

Insert shock. Awe. Jaw hitting the floor.

We received the car back less than a week later without a bill. I didn't just get lucky. I received grace.

Up until this point, I always thought of grace in terms of a conversion—turning your heart to Christ—but now I had discovered a different kind of grace:
The warranty of everyday grace.

"Grace" remains difficult to define. Jesus, someone who talks about it often, never gives us a textbook meaning. Instead, he tells stories about what grace looks like. Even Philip Yancey, someone who wrote one of the most popular books on the subject, calls grace "the most *perplexing*, powerful force in the universe."[11]

Perhaps the simplest definition I've come across is "undeserved love and mercy." Grace emanates from God onto humanity like Niagara Falls, but we're instructed to turn on our faucets and pour the gift on others, too.

When you think about grace only in terms of salvation, you receive your allotment in one scoop. The apostle Peter, has a more expansive (and expanding) understanding:

"Therefore, dear friends, since you have been forewarned, be on your guard so that you may not be carried away by the error of the lawless and fall from your secure position. But grow in the grace and knowledge of our Lord and Savior Jesus Christ" (2 Peter 3:17–18).

 God doesn't dole out grace in one lump sum; he extends it in ever-expanding dividends.

If you are pursuing life as God intends, Peter says you'll live on guard, being careful not to fall under the influence of those who don't play life by God's rules. Instead, you'll grow in grace.

Inch by inch.
Day by day.
Word by word.
Action by action.

Humans are not built like automobiles. We may often feel empty of grace, but we are never too full of it either. God wants to pour ever more into us so that we are saturated by his love and mercy, accompanied by the awareness that we don't deserve a droplet.

Just as God wants to fill our lives with grace with others' help, so, too, he wants to use us to pour grace into the world. We must become conduits of grace.

The people you encounter may not deserve your love or kindness, but they are covered by the warranty of everyday grace. Just as you are. And that is good news, indeed.

FLOURISH TODAY: On a pad next to your bed or in the "Notes" app on your phone, record ways you've received grace each day. Set an alarm to do this each evening for one week. Begin to see the everyday warranty of grace you receive. Reflect on how to dole that out to those around you.

THIS WEEK'S PRAYER: *Father, Thanks for covering my life from bumper to bumper under your warranty of grace. Amen.*

Week 22

WHEN LIFE DOESN'T ADD UP

Have you ever been at the grocery store when the bustling lines to the checkout clerks stretch all the way back down the aisles?

Everyone jockeys for position with nowhere to go. Then a cashier appears out of nowhere, grabs someone at the back of the line, and flips on the light for check stand three. Some lucky soul in the back of the line steps to the front.

If you've been waiting, the annoyance bristles your spine as you race through the gauntlet for the new cashier's line. Few things are more disheartening than realizing that you've waited patiently in line and someone somehow has reversed the order.

If that has ever happened to you, then you know exactly how the audience who heard Jesus' story of the vineyard workers felt.

In Matthew 20, Jesus paints a picture of grace that attracts and repels, inspires and infuriates. He compares the kingdom of heaven to an employer in a down economy. The employer ventures out at daybreak to hire a sidewalk full of day laborers.

Everyone who lands a spot abounds with gratitude, recognizing the work as gift, a provision in tough times. The pay the employer provides is more than most laborers earn in a day. Not only was this a job, but a good one.

Later that morning, the employer returns to hire more laborers. This turns out to be too few. In the afternoon, he makes additional treks to pick up more workers for his vineyards.

The latecomers join the early risers and the half-timers and work the rest of the day.

With the sun melting into the horizon, the final whistle blows. Pay day.

The employer instructs the laborers to line up, first with those who began late in the afternoon all the way down to those who had been working since early in the day. But something strange happens: Each receives the same payment.

The workers who worked the longest hours grow red-faced—not just from the sweltering sun, but from seeing those who never broke a sweat receive the same reward.

Who can blame them?

Few things are worse than putting in your time, paying your dues, refining your craft, then watching someone else skate through to receive the same reward.

In modern day, we have names for people who don't pay their dues— schmoozers and moochers, freeloaders and leeches.

The story Jesus tells rubs us raw when it comes to fairness. Those of us raised with a reinforced work ethic throw up a little in the back of our mouth.

Even worse, Jesus tells the last-minute laborers they will also be paid *first*.

This is like a person who gets catapulted to the front of the grocery line *and then* receives their groceries at a huge discount. Anger and jealousy boil in our chests. We want to call for the store manager for justice. Something has gone terribly wrong.

Jesus scrambles our standard order of things, our innate sense of equity. In the parable, the landowner responds to the workers' complaints:

"I am not being unfair to you, friend. Didn't you agree to work for a denarius? Take your pay and go. I want to give the one who was hired last the same as I gave you. Don't I have the right to do what I want with my own money? Or are you envious because I am generous?'" (Matthew 20:13–15).

Here Jesus explains that God's calculations differ from human math.

In God's economy of grace, two plus two doesn't equal four.

 The algorithms of grace are extravagant.

Deep down none of us really wants two plus two to equal four because if it does then we have to subtract:

God's grace,

God's generosity,

God's love,

God's forgiveness,

God's peace,

God's joy,

and so much more ...

When 2 + 2 = 4, then:

We live as if everything depends on us.
We surround ourselves with rulers and measuring sticks.
We must always negotiate with God and others.
We subtract grace.

One day we're at the front of the line and the next, we're in back. But no one leaves empty-handed, and God never fails to deliver what he promises. God is just and so much more. God generously doles out grace.

God's math zeroes out in fairness and multiplies in bounty. And for that, we can all be grateful.

FLOURISH TODAY: Do some kingdom math. Where are you most grateful God didn't give you what you deserve?

THIS WEEK'S PRAYER: *Father, Help me be grateful for your generous grace no matter where I feel I wound up in line today. Amen.*

THE PHARISEE IN ME

Whenever I read about the Pharisees, I insert the name of a nemesis in place of the Pharisee. This is a nasty habit, but thinking about how they are like Jesus' famed opponents makes me feel better about disliking them.

During the first century, the Pharisees ranked among the most vocal and influential of four major schools of thought within Judaism. The name, Pharisee, in Hebrew means "the separated ones."

Because of their commitment to live according to the Law of Moses and the Prophets, the Pharisees created elaborate rules that kept them from getting anywhere close to smashing an actual commandment of God. These religious leaders were quick to condemn anyone who ruptured one of their commands—including Jesus.

The Gospel of Luke describes the Pharisees as becoming hostile and lying in wait to catch Jesus "in something he might say" (Luke 11:54).

Yet, here, it's the Messiah who finds fault with the faultfinders and exposes their hypocrisy.

This is the point in the story when I celebrate. If Jesus calls out the Pharisees, then he calls out that person I cannot stand, too. In my own telling of the story, I am on Jesus' side, of course.

What makes Pharisaism all the subtler is that it was not blatant legalism that everyone saw through. The Pharisees were the most popular of the

Jewish leadership sects. Their goal was to specify God's will for every conceivable area of life so Jews could know exactly how to please God and respond. When Jesus accused them of hypocrisy, the crowds would have been shocked.

We tend to distance ourselves from the Pharisees, but a close, personal look always reveals the Pharisee in me.

A study by Barna Research reveals the presence of self-righteousness among those who follow Jesus.[12]

The research found that more than half of self-identified Christians in the United States were characterized by having attitudes and actions identified as pharisaical. Only one out of seven Christians responded with the actions and attitudes consistent with Jesus.

The report featured Christlike statements like:

_____ I believe God is for everyone.

_____ I see God working in people's lives, even when they are not following him.

I thought, *That's me!*

Then I studied the remarks used to assess the self-righteous:

_____ I find it hard to be friends with people who seem to constantly do the wrong things.

_____ It's not my responsibility to help people who won't help themselves.

_____ I believe we should stand against those who are opposed to Christian values.

_____ People who follow God's rules are better than those who do not.[13]

My head drops every time I read that list. *That's me, too.*

What about you?

By nature, we can look down our noses at someone else's legalism long before we recognize the tendency in ourselves. But perhaps we shouldn't be surprised by the enticement of legalism.

Strict adherence to a set of rules reduces our murky world to black and white where we don't have to wrestle or humanize an issue.

**When we act like Pharisees,
we become obstacles rather than conduits of grace.**

Taking on a pharisaical attitude will stunt your spiritual growth double-time. If you want to flourish, learn to grow in grace by looking for ways to lighten the load of others.

Growth in grace means we learn to be honest with ourselves and hold off on judging others. Instead of sizing someone up, we can choose to serve.

When we decide to live in grace, we accept that we are as imperfect as the next person.

Learning to grow in grace is not a journey we take on our own. God goes before us and turns our *woes* to *whoas*.

FLOURISH TODAY: Pick one person you've had a harsh, Pharisee-like attitude toward. Find a way to lighten their load through extravagant grace this week.

THIS WEEK'S PRAYER: *Father, Help me identify three areas where I've become Pharisee-like and three ways I can show love and grace instead. Amen.*

Week 24
SILHOUETTES OF GRACE

My friend Carol has anchored my life for decades. She listens and loves me on my most basket-case days. She's my venturesome friend who'll take my call at midnight to help me hide the body—no questions asked.

Because we lived near each other in Colorado, she had a key to our house. When we were out of town, she'd throw parties. Our garage was a storehouse for her friends' cars and our pantry was her eleventh-hour grocery store. Whenever a snack went missing, I giggled and thought of her.

Carol had a longstanding habit of leaving random items in our home. Her clothes hung in our guest bedroom closet. Her hiking shoes parked in our entryway. Three of her water bottles rested in our pantry. She kept a bag or two of who-knows-what in our garage.

Every season, I collected a pile of Carolness next to the front door and stuffed everything in her car when she wasn't looking to ensure the items returned to her home.

Somehow pieces of Carolness never completely disappeared.

Though I'm tempted to find Carol's behavior bothersome, I regard her habit endearing. Why? Carol grew up without a home of her own.

Raised in an orphanage, she didn't have a traditional mother or father. Over the years, Leif and I had the privilege of becoming a home, a family, to her. I now see the items Carol left behind as treasures of love, badges of belonging, symbols of safety.

Growing in grace means considering the whole story of those we meet, encounter, and befriend. Grace changes the lens through which we see life. But acquiring grace often means asking questions and mining a person's past.

Without the backstory, we can make decrees regarding people's motives, responses, and appearances as if everyone we encounter are contestants waiting to be voted off the island.

 When you discover the untold story, you discover God's unfolding glory.

As we learn other people's stories, we discover silhouettes of grace surrounding us.

We're invited to strap on our grace goggles, dig deeper, ask questions, and grow in relationship. Soon, we catch glimpses of these graceful silhouettes that have surrounded us unnoticed.

In 2 Corinthians 8:7 Paul writes, "But since you excel in everything— in faith, in speech, in knowledge, in complete earnestness and in the love we have kindled in you—see that you also excel in this grace of giving."

Giving is often measured in terms of pocketbooks and accounting ledgers. But grace invites us to give more than money. Growing in grace requires us to give the benefit of the doubt and offer a second chance to

the best friend who betrays,
the spouse whose addiction destroys the family,
the coworker who one-ups,
the rude neighbor whose Great Dane relieves himself in your yard.

The temptation to skimp on grace arises when we see a teenage girl
whose outfit consists of less material than our skivvies. Or the sales clerk
who seems to move slow on purpose. Or the coworker who ignores
deadlines leaving everyone else to work late nights. Or the family
members whose impossible expectations for holiday gatherings
are never met.

Grace invites us to scope for where God is flourishing—not only in
the present, but also in the past. Not just in our lives, but in the lives of
others, too.

How our perspective shifts when we see

the perseverance of the mother with the tired toddler,
the overload of the professor ignoring your email,
the insecurity of the rude teenager,
the tenderness of the weepy, weary friend.

These are moments for pardon, not prudery. What can we possibly
dictate to those who are teetering in that place of flourishing where
the hard and the heavy meet heaven's heart?

God flourishes, pushes his shoots up, even through soil compacted
down by the pacing of worried feet. He turns the dark and shadowed
seedling, and brings new life and light.

Grace gives us eyes to see the living miracles all around that stretch from the first chapter of someone's story to the final closing word. We don't write that story. We simply read and look for the silhouette of grace.

FLOURISH TODAY: Select two friends whose backstories you don't know. Pick up the phone and set dates on the calendar to learn more about them.

THIS WEEK'S PRAYER: *Father, Give me patience with those I meet mid-story. Amen.*

Pray & Reflect

But since you excel in everything—in faith, in speech,
in knowledge, in complete earnestness
and in the love we have kindled in you—see that you
also excel in this grace of giving.

2 Corinthians 8:7

Prepared for Drought

Week 25
TREASURES OF THE WILDERNESS

The Bible bestows a name on places marked by drought: wilderness. Several years ago, I traveled to Israel and experienced the famed terrain firsthand.

The tan, rocky hills sat bleak. The dryness gave birth to a litter of dust. The heat suffocated and depleted. If I stood in the sun too long, I pressed my body against the side of our filthy van to snatch a hint of shade.

The biblical word *eremos* means "desert wilderness." Being there doesn't just make you feel parched, but also isolated. The barren expanse can force even the extreme introvert to sense loneliness. This characteristic surprises considering God often leads his people into this desolate place on purpose.

The Israelites, Jesus, even Paul trekked to and through the wilderness because God led them there.

Of all the wilderness dwellers, John the Baptist ranks among the most beloved. While wealthy men wore wool and ornate belts, John enrobed himself in the clothes of the poor—scratchy camel hair wrapped with a thick leather belt.[14]

This man soon became a spiritual tourist attraction. Men and women backpacked into the wilderness to see this strange wanderer who pioneered one of the first and least popular versions of the Whole 30 diet.

From his backcountry pulpit, John stands among those known as "fire and brimstone" preachers. He delivers the same sermon:

"Repent, for the kingdom of heaven has come near" (Matthew 3:2).

Jesus echoes the same sermon, often delivered in the wilderness, too: "Repent, for the kingdom of heaven has come near" (Matthew 4:17).

That's an interesting word, "repent." The Greek word *metanoia* means "to change one's mind." Repentance never plops on the chaise lounge, munches on sea-salt kettle chips, binge watching HGTV. Instead, repentance romps around, moving and morphing, poking and prodding us nearer to God.

Why does it matter that the message of repentance is preached in the wilderness? Because the lonely expanse of the wilderness allows room for preparation, development, maturation. When you're in the wilderness, never forget:

 God cares more about your character than your comfort.

God's boot camp occurs in the desert: double-time marches through the sand, belly crawls into rocky bunkers, minimal rations. Though we rail against the sand and rocks, blistered and burned, this place of hiddenness provides a training ground for transformation.

Perhaps we should not be surprised that the terrain for God's declaration, "See, I am doing a new thing!" (Isaiah 43:19) is the wilderness and the wasteland.

God leading you into a drought-marked desert to grow you seems counterintuitive, because little grows in the desert. Yet the emptiness, the loneliness, delivers us to a place where all the distractions and falsities of self-sufficiency are sand-blasted away. We must turn to God, to repent, and to rely on God for provision and protection. In the wilderness, God moves, works and transforms. God grows hardy children in the wasteland.[15]

If you find yourself in a time of drought, forced to bake in life's rocky wilderness, take heart.

Bare doesn't mean barren with God's presence.

FLOURISH TODAY: Identify a specific area of your life that needs to be transformed. How can you begin the process of repentance to change your mind regarding that situation?

THIS WEEK'S PRAYER: *Father, Change my mind, lead me to repent of my sins, reveal the hidden treasures of the wilderness, and teach me to trust you in the drought. Amen.*

Week 26
FOUND IN HIDDENNESS

I know a little something about the desert. After all, I live in one.

Many people don't think about Salt Lake City, Utah, in the same way they think about the Sahara. But don't be tricked. Utah ranks the second driest state in the United States, just behind Nevada.

Whenever we are thrust into a desert—whether geographical, professional, spiritual, emotional—we must learn new skills to survive. Even in our short time here, I'm convinced the desert is one of the most stunning places that we have ever lived.

Even when my nose is chalky with sunburn.
Even when my lips crack.
Even when I lose my way.
Even when I want to give up.

The desert is not just a place of isolation but of hiddenness. The vastness of the desert can make you feel unimportant, unseen, invisible.

Entering the desert, we transition from being sought out to being left out, from being remembered to forgotten, from being noticed to being unseen.

Sometimes we enter this terrain on purpose as we take the next step in our career or move to live closer to the grandkids.

Sometimes we are thrust into a deeper desert by no choice of our own. A life-threatening diagnosis or the grief following the death of a child plunges us into a place where no one knows us anymore.

People may catch glimpses of our fight and our plight, but few seem to understand life as a desert dweller. We wave our arms like someone stranded on an island attempting to flag down a passing ship, but no one seems to notice.

Hiddenness played a key role in the life of Christ. No human sees him overcome temptation and the devil in the desert. Only a handful of humans witness his transfiguration in the desert. Jesus spends time in prayer with the Father in the desert. In each of these moments, Jesus lives hidden away.

In John 6:15, Jesus sees that his life could take a very wrong turn when the crowd pushes to crown him king "by force." He responds by escaping, hiding, allowing the passion to pass. This serves as a turning point. Jesus' hiddenness confirmes his character. He is the Bread of Life, not a rising rebel.

If hiddenness playes a role in Jesus' life, it will play a role in ours, too. Remember: As followers of Jesus, we go where he goes. This means we will, at some point, end up hidden in the desert.

I don't know what kind of hiddenness you find yourself in. Your journey might be marked by:

Loneliness.

Isolation.

Failure.

Exhaustion.

Injury.

Silence.

Hardship.

Adversity.

Rejection.

Discomfort.

Regardless, Christ sees these struggles and invites you deeper into his:

Strength.

Healing.

Arms.

Love.

Oceanic grace.

Mercy.

 When you enter a season of hiddenness, remember the One who still sees you.

The writer of Hebrews encourages, "Nothing in all creation is hidden from God's sight. Everything is uncovered and laid bare before the eyes of him to whom we must give account" (4:13).

Time in the desert often precedes movement toward a place of deep springs and dew-dabbed grass. Places where we know and perceive once again that we are sought, remembered, and noticed by God. Uncovered and laid bare, we rise with new confidence that God knows, God hears, God sees.

And those whom God sees, God also saves.

In his greatest desert trial on the cross, Jesus cried out to his Father, "My God, my God! Why have You forsaken me?" (Matthew 27:46). It was the cry of the psalmist, too, "Why are you so far from saving me, so far from my cries of anguish?" (Psalm 22:1).

God saw and God saved, not just his only Son who became a risen Lord, but all of us.

FLOURISH TODAY: Read Genesis 16. Take note of the story of Hagar. How has God used the hidden years of your life to transform you and make you more fruitful?

THIS WEEK'S PRAYER: *Father, Thank you for seeing me when I feel invisible and helping me when I feel abandoned. Amen.*

Week 27

THE BEAST OF TEMPTATION

I'm a glutton for building memories with friends, often at my own peril. In an effort to *carpe diem*, I become *carpe dum-dum*.

I stay awake until 3:00 a.m. chatting away, refusing to calculate the toll on my health, work, and relationships the following day.

I shoehorn loads of activities into vacations and return home more exhausted then when I left.

Eying an open slot on the calendar, I think, *I can squish that in*, without seeing the bigger picture of all I've already scheduled.

I'm prone to value quantity over quality, busyness over rest, distraction over presence.

One story of Jesus in the desert resonates deep with my roadrunner–like pace. Meep. Meep. In Luke's Gospel, Jesus winds up in the desert: "Then Jesus, full of the Holy Spirit, returned from the Jordan River. He was led by the Spirit in the wilderness, where he was tempted by the devil for forty days" (Luke 4:1-2 NLT).

The Spirit guides Jesus' every step into a barren, seared land where the Son of God bakes for forty days and shivers for forty nights. All before the devil tempts him on an empty stomach.

The Holy Spirit's involvement in the ordeal seems peculiar until we remember that as with other stories in Scripture, the desert turns out to be a training ground for spiritual growth.

The devil makes a three-fold effort to tempt Jesus, beginning with a slab of bread from the best bakery in town. "If you are the Son of God, tell this stone to become bread," says the dark one (Luke 4:3).

The Bible never reveals the kind of bread the stones might have sprouted. Perhaps buttery-hot croissants. Melt-in-your mouth biscuits. Roasted-olive focaccia. Pomegranate pancakes drizzled with fig syrup.

Jesus doesn't bite—*see what I did there*—and refutes with a powerful passage instead, "One does not live by bread alone" (Deuteronomy 8:3; Luke 4:4 NRSV).

Jesus' resistance doesn't center on gluttony of food, but the temptation to save oneself by one's own work rather than depend on God. The Bread of Life resists the urge to do and perform.

The devil circles back and this time leads Jesus—notice the Spirit doesn't lead here—to a high place to survey all the kingdoms of the world. The temptation: Worship the adversary in exchange for possession and control. Some interpret this temptation as a thinly veiled shortcut around the cross.

Jesus refutes with another Scripture: "Worship the Lord your God and serve him only" (Luke 4:8).

The King of kings resists the urge to possess and control.

In a final attempt, the devil leads Jesus to Jerusalem. The adversary asks Jesus to verify he is the Son of God by jumping off the pinnacle of the temple.

Jesus challenges with yet another potent Scripture: "Do not put the Lord your God to the test" (Deuteronomy 6:16; Luke 4:12).

The Living Word resists the urge to prove and accomplish.

The devil disappears and waits in the shadows for a more suitable time.

We all have core struggles and central battles that intensify during seasons of drought. Even if you cannot name yours, they likely fall into the same categories of temptations Jesus faced:

The urge to do and perform.
The urge to possess and control.
The urge to prove and accomplish.

Jesus' victory over the adversary in the desert reminds us that God always provides an escape hatch when it comes to temptation: "When you are tempted, he will also provide a way out so that you can endure" (1 Corinthians 10:13).

Being prepared for drought means we can expect that sooner or later we will be allured. Remember:

Temptations will try to bring out the worst in you, but they don't have to get the best of you.

FLOURISH TODAY: Identify three temptations in your life. Then develop a three-prong plan to fortify your life from these temptations.

THIS WEEK'S PRAYER: *Father, Show me where I'm being tempted to do and perform, possess and control, prove and accomplish. Give me the strength and strategies to overcome and live in obedience to you. Amen.*

Week 28
THE ART OF REMEMBRANCE

Do you recall ancient Israel's history?

After years of brutal slavery, God hand-selects a Hebrew shepherd with a shady past named Moses to bring liberation to his people. Through a spate of miracles, God demonstrates his power over the thousands of gods of ancient Egypt.

The Nile turns to blood. Frogs, gnats, and flies multiply. Animals collapse. Skin oozes. Hail and locusts obliterate vegetation. Light disappears into darkness. All lose their firstborn sons except those who mark their doors with the blood of the lamb.

The wake of devastation topples the Egyptian gods and turns Pharaoh's heart. God's people must leave. In holy terror and awe, the Egyptians stuff the Israelite's luggage with gold and silver—jewelry, trinkets, nuggets, flakes, even gods—as well as their clothing. God's people do not depart empty-handed.[16]

Pharaoh's heart soon turns back to stone. He sends 600 chariots of soldiers to chase down more than 600,000 Jews. Despite the long odds, the Israelites find themselves trapped between the Red Sea and the impending army.

Gripped with fear, the Israelites frenzy and yelp at God.

"Was it because there were no graves in Egypt that you brought us to the desert to die?" the Israelites bellow. "What have you done to us by bringing us out of Egypt?" (Exodus 14:11-12).

With Pharaoh in pursuit, the promises of God vaporize from their memory. The Israelites have forgotten that difficult positions do not limit divine potential in their lives.[17]

Though blindsided by the Israelites' rickety faith, Moses instructs the people not to fear. He grounds them in the promises of God and instructs, "the Lord will fight for you *while you keep silent*" (Exodus 14:14 NASB).

Then Moses stretches his hands over the waters. The seabed emerges as dry land. The Israelites make their way across, careful not to catch their sandals on the coral.

The Egyptians pursue. When they realize God is fighting on behalf of the Israelites, they flee in terror—right into the heart of the sea that crashes down on them with a thunderous roar. The Egyptian army is gone, baby, gone.

Such an epic story appears impossible to forget. Yet the Hebrew people soon experience spiritual amnesia. In three winks, they complain and gripe and doubt the Lord will come through. Their forty years as desert dwellers are marked by whining.

It's easy to judge the Hebrew people from our vantage point. We have the whole story—both the tragedies and triumphs—just a few pages away. But the Israelites had to work at remembering these events.

For this reason, God makes sure that stories of his deliverance shape their celebrations and sacred rituals. Their songs speak of the God of salvation who leads them to and through the wilderness. Their history recounts the warrior God who set them free, the Lord who reigns forever and ever. Their holy chorus echoes with praise, adoration, thanksgiving.[18]

Time and time again throughout Scripture, God instructs the Israelites to remember their salvation and rescue. God's people must tell and retell these stories from generation to generation.

Gathered around campfires.
Celebrated at feasts.
Remembered before bed.
Voiced through poem and song.

For those in the midst of drought or desert dwelling, remembrance provides an essential spiritual discipline.

 **Remembrance recalls the past
and propels us toward a faith-filled future.**

Why is this crucial? Droughts and deserts bait you to forget.

Dust clouds the long-range view. Relief from the intense heat sears every thought. Hope and vibrancy soon wilt.

These places can make you think that the desolation is where you have been, where you are, and where you will remain forever.

The desert tempts us to wallow in the present, but God calls us into the past to infuse us with hope for the future. We must call to mind those moments of God's faithfulness, competence, and miraculous rescue. We must remember God never changes, if he has rescued us in the past, he will again.

When you question God's faithfulness, remember. Recall all those times he has proved himself true in the past and hope for all the times he will do so in the future.

FLOURISH TODAY: Journal about a time of dire circumstance when God showed up and rescued you.

THIS WEEK'S PRAYER: *Father, Help me to notice your provision in the present and never forget your provision in the past and give me hope for the future. Amen.*

Pray & Reflect

When you
are
tempted

he will also
provide
a way out

so that you
can
endure.

1 Corinthians
10:13

Protected
from
Floods

Week 29

THE FLOOD OF BUSYNESS

In life's busiest moments, we morph from a human being into a human doing. Our bodies, minds, relationships, and spiritual well-being takes a heavy toll as ignoring God's rhythms of rest can lead to state of exhaustion and burnout.

The busyness, the go-go-go, the intensity. We rush through our routines, never stopping, never slowing. Then we realize we're empty. Breathless. Spent.

I know because all too often I find myself drowning in the flood of busyness.

My husband, Leif, recently noted how my stuffed schedule was taking a low-grade toll on me. My life bounced between email accounts, texts, conference calls, creative team consultations, writing, research, and an all-day online seminar.

Surrounded by stacks of projects and deadlines that all needed to be done yesterday, I felt rattled inside. Meanwhile, working from home blurred the line between professional and personal as any entrepreneur or self-employed person will tell you.

Plus, one friend was in intense therapy, another unloading a moving truck. I wanted to help and support both. I felt tugged in a dozen different directions—work, help, respond, pray, connect, repeat.

The list of to-dos buzzed like a mosquito in my ear.

Any of this sound familiar?

Busyness demands that we flit between many projects—both professional and personal—though nothing ever feels complete.

Busyness promises a sense of achievement, but delivers an ache of emptiness.

Worse, busyness doesn't stay in one place. Busyness bleeds through any boundaries, like toddler fingers that wiggle under the bathroom door while you're taking a minute for yourself.

Given enough time, busyness floods our relationships. We schedule much-valued time with a close friend, and then BOOM. Busyness swoops in with the melody of a cell phone ring.

"Say that one more time," we tell our friend while we text another. We try to appear extra interested but haven't heard a word.

Busyness floods into our relationship with God as well. We sit down to pray or study and within two minutes busyness signals us toward the laundry room or the compounding inbox.

 Busyness makes a brutal taskmaster.

What starts as a trickle of tasks soon becomes a deluge.

Jesus knows this, which is why he invites his disciples, "Come with me by yourselves to a quiet place and get some rest" (Mark 6:31).

Do you want to withdraw with Jesus to a sleepy place and imbibe rest?

If so, you must discover what's causing your deep-seated need for overproduction.

Then you must cut your excess, reduce your waste, and learn to be more fully present.

I have a hunch we both need to practice a spiritual frugality whereby we do less in order to experience more with God and those we love. Such a practice seems counterintuitive but helps us discover absurd happiness in the details of life.

The resistance against mindless busyness and the quest to enjoy life, fully present and undistracted, invites us to jettison the notion that our only value consists in our performance and accomplishments.

Detaching from productivity and doing is hard for me. Yet when I turn off the computer, close the door to the laundry room, and withdraw from life, I begin to reawaken to the presence of God and the wonder of life.

When I say no to busyness, I rediscover the sweetness of my relationship with Leif. Laughter with friends flows more freely. I drink in the radiance of more sunrises and sunsets. Joy percolates in my heart. I wake up rested rather than exhausted.

In resisting busyness, we can once again restake our claim as wholly loved by God and flourish in the joy of being his children. This frees us from the bondage of overproduction and liberates us; our hearts lie fallow to receive God's goodness and grace.

FLOURISH TODAY: Mind your Ps and Qs—your peace and quiet. Take five minutes to get away and enjoy the silence and stillness of God's presence.

THIS WEEK'S PRAYER: *Father, Save me from my busyness. Amen.*

Week 30
DOWNPOURS OF DISTRACTION

Life seemed fuzzy around the edges.

At the grocery store, I'd look at the shelves with a blank stare having forgotten what I came in to purchase. On one work-trip I forgot to pack pants; another I forgot undergarments. I misplaced credit cards, checkbooks, and my cell phone at least a dozen times. My sunglasses kept disappearing... on top of my head.

A quick visit to the doctor revealed I was in good health, but my friends couldn't resist second-guessing the diagnosis. They lovingly suggested I suffered from Dory syndrome, named after the fictional fish in *Finding Dory* who struggles with short-term memory loss.

I was doing far too many things at once and none of them well.

If busyness is running from task to task, then scatterbrained is not making the connection between all of your tasks. Instead of flourishing, I weakened amidst the downpour of distraction.

I always suspected my phone was a source of disruption; I just never knew how big of a source. The incoming rings and buzzes and bings trained me to turn to my phone for a boost. Some days I reach for information; other days I reach for connection; still others, I reach for a laugh.

I turned to my phone as if were a slot machine, a place of escape that might dispense pleasure. Pushing the buttons was like an instant trip to

Vegas, a bid for a little "win," rather than the choice to be present, more focused in the moment.

This little device cost me a gradual inattention that eroded my mental life and my spiritual life. The multitude of distractions blinded and numbed me to God's presence and made me more prone to diversion by the next object that caught my attention.

The downpour of distractions in life can drive us batty. More than a bad habit it can become an addiction.

 Distraction sells immediate abundance but delivers long-term unfruitfulness.

Like all addictions, distraction comes with a heavy cost. The allure of faster and more makes me run toward the elusive sense of pleasure that masquerades as fulfillment and meaning. But it always ends in a cul-de-sac of shallowness and stress.

Living overstimulated and underfocused saps your mind, emotions, soul, and relationships. This can even keep you from accomplishing God's mission for your life. You can become deaf to the cries of those in need, blind to the sight of those in poverty, numb to the news of those living in injustice.

After talking with Leif about my addiction to distractions, I decided to incorporate an ancient prayer practice into my life. Drawn from one of the most famous verses in the Bible:

"Be still, and know that I am God" (Psalms 46:10).

Whenever I feel scatterbrained, whenever I can't seem to concentrate, whenever my Dory syndrome flares up, I pause. I breathe slowly, concentrate, and count my inhales and exhales. A few breaths in, I whisper the words of the psalmist, then I take another breath and speak the next word.

Be.

Be still.

Be still and.

Be still and know.

Be still and know that.

Be still and know that I.

Be still and know that I am.

Be still and know that I am God.

By the time the word "God" leaves my lips, I feel calm and laser focused. I feel more centered on God, resting in his embrace. I am stilled by the knowledge of God's God-ness. I begin to flourish right where I am— in the midst of the distractions.

As you learn to focus on what's important, say no to lesser priorities and be more intentional about your connection with God, borrow this prayer and make it your own. May you rest present in God's presence.

FLOURISH TODAY: Take time today to drink in the silence and pray the "Be Still" prayer.

THIS WEEK'S PRAYER: *Father, Hold me still and close to you. Amen.*

Week 31

THE TORRENT OF MULTITASKING

Busyness gives birth to the dastardliest offspring: multitasking.

Multitasking is nothing new. Humans have a capacity for attending
to several activities at once. Without this capability, most of my mommy
friends would never survive. Try asking the parent of a two-year-old
to stop multitasking and do only one thing at a time, then let me know
when they stop laughing.

We have grown accustomed to performing basic tasks in tandem. We
talk on the phone while folding laundry or pull weeds from the front
lawn while catching up with a neighbor. We don't even notice how
many plates spin simultaneously.

But in the last two decades multitasking has reached warp speed with
web-enabled devices that allow us to watch a live episode of a talent
competition, vote online for our favorite performer, check tomorrow's
weather, message with a long-distance friend, score a pair of jeans on
sale, reach the next level of Candy Crush Saga, and reload our Starbucks
card all at the same time.

We forget that fifteen years ago most home computers weren't linked
to the Internet. Way back in the early 1990s, a group of adolescents
were surveyed about which device they couldn't live without. The vast
majority said a radio or CD player. Ah, those were the days. [19]

Technological changes have arrived so fast that scientists are still
assessing the comprehensive impact on our lives.

Some of us have convinced ourselves that we're good at multitasking, a few might even classify ourselves as rock stars.

A group of undergraduates at the University of Utah were asked to rate their ability to multitask on a scale of 0 to 100, and then tested for their ability to do so. The researchers discovered that those who deemed themselves the best multitaskers were the least effective.[20]

We are not as efficient as we believe.

This kind of arrogance doesn't just take a heavy toll on the quality of our work but the quality of our connections with others.

We begin shortchanging people by being late and not fully present when we arrive. The practice of multitasking doesn't just stop at the end of the workday—it follows us home. We may be in the same room with our spouse or children or friends, but we're not there. Our mind lingers on a task left undone or an email that needs to be sent. If left unchecked, we can wake up one day and realize we've lived blind and deaf to those we love most.

Multitasking shapes me into a flutterby, someone who circles everything but lands on nothing. Some days Leif will ask me, "What did you do today?"

"Nothing and everything," I answer.

Those are the days the tasks I savor transform into chores. That's when I'm most likely to treat people like objects, and lose sight of my human limits that are meant to keep me in touch with God. If left unchecked, hurry becomes a survival skill for my frenetic life.

Jesus knows the temptation of multitasking, too. In Mark 1, he finishes a stretch of healing people with a multitude of sicknesses. Exhausted from the long day, Jesus needs to retreat for some alone time in prayer.

The disciples locate him: "Everyone is looking for you!" (Mark 1:37).

In other words, "There is much work to be done, pal. People need to be healed, demons need to be cast out, miracles need to be performed." But Jesus does not allow himself to be distracted by anything—not even good things.

"We must go on to other towns as well, and I will preach to them, too. That is why I came," Jesus replies (Mark 1:38, NLT).

Jesus' day floods with a myriad of demands, but he resists the temptation to be sidetracked by everyone. Others need to see him and hear him preach. He has a limited time to accomplish his task, and he did not allow others' expectations to control him.

Yet Jesus understood the importance of prioritizing and knew what was most important to his mission. He only did what he saw the Father doing (John 5:19).

 Sometimes we must retreat in order to advance.

When we find ourselves swept away by the torrent of multitasking, we can draw from Jesus' example. Not every item on your to-do list needs to be done today, right now, this minute. Even good actions sometimes need to wait.

Give yourself permission today to step back, slow down, and do one thing at a time.

FLOURISH TODAY: Choose to do one activity at a time throughout the day. Pay attention to how your renewed focus affects your relationships and level of stress.

THIS WEEK'S PRAYER: *Father, Help me to rediscover the joys of scaled-back simplicity. Amen.*

Week 32
CLOUDLESS AND CLEAR SKIES

We can't talk about distractions and busyness and multitasking apart from the composition of technology. The screens and ware and computer devices we use are designed to make us pay attention to them and nothing else.

They become the center of our lives through brain science: "New information creates a rush of dopamine to the brain, a neurotransmitter that makes you feel good… The promise of new information compels your brain to seek out that dopamine rush."[21]

Every ding—Facebook, Twitter, Instagram, email, text—floods my brain with dopamine. The rush instigates behaviors that reinforce my desires. Immediate response soon becomes habit.

Start a project. Need dopamine. Check Facebook. Dopamine rush. Check email. Second dopamine rush. Hit refresh. No new emails. Visit Twitter for dopamine rush. Return to project. Repeat cycle again and again.

No wonder it's so hard not to look at our phones when we feel the vibration or hear the ping. Our brain urges, "You want this. Take a peek." We become connected to its call, servants of the surge.

Though our devices are wireless, all too often they cord us to

the expectations of others,
commitments we regret,
life-sucking activities,
unhealthy bonds.

These ties undermine our ability to thrive over the long haul. These ropes reduce our fruitfulness, and the strings stunt our long-term growth.

Survival in the downpour of incoming data requires us to unplug from time to time. Resist the dopamine. Reshape our brain chemistry by slowing to drink in the wonder of creation and hear the crinkle of the pages of Scripture.

Sometimes I'll tuck my phone into my bedside drawer for a day of techno rest. If the temptation to retrieve the device is too strong, I'll ask Leif to hide my phone from me. I need help in escaping the deluge of data and resetting my priorities.

Yet a single day without a phone does the soul good.

The Gospel of Matthew beckons us deeper into the life of Christ. Jesus *calls out, gives out,* then *sends out* "his twelve" to *drive out* and heal every disease and sickness (Matthew 10:1).

Soon after Jesus offers an invitation that sticks like Velcro on my soul:

"Come to me, all you who are weary and burdened, and I will give you rest. Take my yoke upon you and learn from me, for I am gentle and humble in heart, and you will find rest for your souls. For my yoke is easy and my burden is light" (Matthew 11:28-30).

In one of his most beloved discourses, the Son of God turns to those who are overworked and weighted down. While technology forms the social sinew of our time, religious practice was the cultural connective tissue of theirs. Jesus addresses the burdens of the religious regulations imposed by their leaders and exhorts them to come, take his yoke.

The yoke was a common way to refer to discipleship; an act of relenting to be made like one's teacher. Young disciples had many rabbis to choose from, whom they had to court before they could commit to study and emulate.

With this invitation, Jesus instructs disciples not to take on the yoke or teaching of the religious leaders that were heavy and burdensome but to take on his yoke, his teaching—one that's marked by love, forgiveness, grace, and rest.

At the core of Jesus' invitation is the question of allegiance. Jesus, invites us into his service where our sense of worth is not based on how many tasks we can accomplish at once or how large our social media platform is, but on him.

Do we respond to every ping and ring? Do we serve the expectations of others? Do we attempt to earn favor with God through our good works?

Or do we follow Jesus and trust him for our fruitfulness?

After he gives the invitation, he treks through a grain field and speaks of Sabbath. Rest is part of the yoke.

This is no coincidence. This holy pause establishes limits that we may need but struggle to impose on ourselves or permit to others. When the dings of data flood our lives and steal our attention, Sabbath offers an invitation to experience cloudless, clear sky.

166

Sabbath is an act of compassion for humanity. This sacred gift—a gift in time and space set apart for us to occupy with God.

A holy pause breaks us free from the unhealthy tethers in our lives, such as:

false beliefs that creep into our thinking.
idols that crawl into our pockets when we're not looking.
blurriness that comes with living too fast.
legalistic choices that slip into our lives.
addictions that feel impressive but leave us imprisoned.

**Sabbath pries our fingers from the earthly
and frees us to lay hold of the eternal.**

The gift of Sabbath liberates us from everything that holds us back and binds us to the One committed to see us flourish.

FLOURISH TODAY: Consider one technological device to which you've corded yourself. Turn it off for twenty-four hours and reset your allegiance to Christ.

THIS WEEK'S PRAYER: *Father, be my number one yokemate. Amen.*

167

Pray & Reflect

Come to me, all you
who are weary and burdened,
and I will give you rest.
Take my yoke upon you
and learn from me, for I am
gentle and humble in heart,
and you will find rest for your souls.
For my yoke is easy
and my burden is light.

MATTHEW 11:28–30

Budding
with
Hope

Week 33
FIND YOUR HOTDOG CART

"Of course he built his own submarine," I laughed.

During the five years Leif and I lived in Alaska, I grew accustomed to hearing strange stories. But this one may have topped them all.

While walking the docks in Juneau, Leif and I encountered a man who had constructed his own submarine complete with a cannon on top. The salty owner said he didn't like shooting the heavy cannonballs too often—they were expensive and hard to retrieve. But on calm days, he enjoyed taking the submarine for an underwater cruise through the harbor nine feet below the surface.

The rugged nature of Alaska brings out people's ingenuity. The remoteness, harsh climate, and lack of resources force people outside any metaphorical boxes. Anyone who spends more than a year in this great state knows that anything is possible if you have duct tape, a blue tarp, and a whim of creativity.

The autumn season proves to be a breeding ground for strange ideas in Alaska. Maybe it's the excessive rain or short days or bracing for winter. Off-beat ideas just pop and crackle like the first log on the fire.

My offbeat idea was to open a hotdog cart in downtown Juneau. I envisioned hawking reindeer sausage dogs to cruise-ship tourists.

My dream never made it further than some late night online research of moose, elk, and wild game suppliers.

Unlike the harbor-exploring submarine builder, I never lived my dream of circling the city gripping a hotdog cart.

Everyone has a rearview mirror that reflects back unrealized dreams littering the roadside. If we are not careful, our disappointments, failures, and regrets can take a heavy toll on our resolve to hope again.

The prophet Isaiah, spoke to a nation that found themselves on a road far from their dreams, exiled in Babylon, conquered, and waiting for God's rescue. To kindle their holy anticipation, Isaiah writes:

"Then you will see this, and your heart will be glad, and your bones will flourish like the new grass" (Isaiah 66:14, NASB).

The prophet provides what an English teacher would call a "mixed metaphor." Bones collide with grass and the result is flourishing. *What? Huh? Come again?*

Modern catch phrases remind us that bones represent the place where we feel. We work our fingers to the bone. We have a bone to pick with someone. We can be bone tired and bone headed. Several psalms describe how our hopeless thoughts and feelings can become so internalized that they settle into our bones.

Medical science reveals that the marrow of our bones produces life—red blood cells surge through our veins oxygenating our bodies. Bones symbolize more than just emotions, but the core lifeline of a person. Bones remain after death—a lasting testimony to someone's existence.

Isaiah's botanical metaphor symbolizes life, as the Bible often does. The prophet speaks of people sprouting among vegetation. Taken together, Isaiah suggests that God will make the emotional cores of his people spring to life.

As you study the Bible, you soon realize that this is what God does.

 God makes fallow fields full, barren women pregnant, dead bones alive again.

When you circle a dream so many times but never cross the threshold of realization—be it a hotdog cart or a fill-in-the-blank—discouragement sets in. We convince ourselves the dream and all that budding of hope is for someone else, anyone else, those build-your-own-submarine-Alaskans—everyone except us.

But Isaiah plants us in the truth that no matter how much hope we've lost or misplaced, God is always doing something new within us.

Even when all your resources are stripped and disappointment has settled in, you can hope in God—who hasn't left you or forgotten you. Don't focus on the unrealized dreams in your rearview mirror. Dare to hope again.

FLOURISH TODAY: Hope is the fertilizer for our lives. Without hope, God's people wither. Pray *with* hope *for* hope.

THIS WEEK'S PRAYER: *Father, Renew hope deep within my bones. Amen.*

Week 34
SPUR HOPE

Lying in bed, my mind wandered to an area of my life aching for more love—my relationship with Leif.

For the past seven months, he had been considering a job opportunity that required us to move to Utah. My friends were in Colorado, as was the life we'd worked hard to build.

Even more than that, I adored having my husband as my co-worker in ministry. For years, we'd been a package deal. Donny and Marie, Simon and Garfunkel, Ken and Barbie, Kenan and Kel, Brad and Angelina. *Have I covered your childhood yet?*

The pairing seemed perfect. Where I wobbled, he remained robust and vice versa. I focused on speaking and writing. He handled the business, travel arrangements, and event book table.

He always ended up being the main attraction because of his magnetic personality and quick wit. Not to mention, less merchandise wanders off with a nearly seven-foot-tall Norwegian on guard.

But for some time, Leif sensed God nudging him into a new season of life to do a different kind of work. I sensed it, too.

Over time, I noticed Leif morph from road warrior to road weary. Instead of breathing life and hope, work left him burnt out and dog-tired.

The position at a church in Utah seemed like an answer to a thousand prayers—health insurance, the opportunity for Leif to use his management skills, and more.

We knew that God was moving us to a space and place where we could both use more of our gifts. Leif had supported me for so long. Now, I could support him and we could learn to dream together. Leif accepted the job in Utah.

Let me be clear: I don't pretend life has been easy since Leif accepted his new position. We had eighteen days to pack and change states. Saying goodbye to our friends-who-had-become-family is never easy. We've had to renegotiate my writing and speaking, our marriage, the rhythms of our new life.

But I've watched Leif come alive in his new role. Most days he's like a boy on Christmas morning when he goes to work. My best friend is now budding with hope and helping others awaken to their gifting and talents. I'm learning to celebrate and appreciate my husband in a whole new way. Meanwhile I'm learning to find new outlets to thrive in my calling, too.

After working together for eight years, much of the lines between life and work blurred. Now, we are becoming intentional to have conversations that don't revolve around work. Together, we're exploring a new city and making new friends. I have the privilege of coming alongside Leif at the church to serve, and Leif still travels with me on a handful of work trips. We're experiencing the tangy fruitfulness of flourishing together.

The writer of the Hebrews challenges:

"Let us consider how we may spur one another on toward love and good deeds" (10:24).

The Greek word for "spur" is *paroxysmos* and suggests a provoking or sharp incitement. In other words, we are to consider how we can electrify the dormant dreams of others that lead to loving, good works. We are to help others flourish as we do the same.

 Electrifying the dreams of others energizes our own God-given dreams.

This isn't just something we do one-on-one; this is a communal act. As we gather together as believers, we are to spur the dreams of others. This requires recognizing hidden potential. Calling out God-instilled gifting. Nudging others to take action and step out in faith.

One of my friends, Jessica, has worked with us for many years. She is an outstanding artist with a gift for handcrafted lettering. Her drawings and doodles have become ever more stunning over the years.

In fact, her work marks the cover of this book. I asked her to create the hand-lettering on the cover of *Flourish*, because I knew she'd create a gorgeous custom work. And I wanted to fan the flame within her of creating beautiful, inspiring works for others.[22]

My hunch is that you know someone right now with a gifting who just needs an infusion of hope and opportunity to grow.

Who do you know that has a dream lying dormant? Who in your life needs a holy nudge, a burst of encouragement and hope to take that first step?

FLOURISH TODAY: Call a friend or family member who comes to mind that you've been holding back. Set them free to follow their dreams without blowback or penalty.

THIS WEEK'S PRAYER: *Father, Reveal areas where I'm preventing others from flourishing. Amen.*

Week 35
HOPE IN WAITING

For many centuries, Christians have proclaimed a three-pronged confession before breaking bread together:

Christ has died.
Christ is risen.
Christ will come again.

One of the great mysteries of following Jesus is that even though he has already come and is coming to us in this very moment, we are always waiting for him to come again.

To follow Jesus is to live "in-between."

This is hopeful news for those of us who are holding our breath, withering with worry, and dreading tomorrow.

In-between jobs.
In-between relationships.
In-between places to live.
In-between paychecks.

Frustrated, you may find yourself crying out to God with the words of the prophet Habakkuk: "How long, LORD, must I call for help, but you do not listen?" (1:2).

The prophet watches God's hand of provision lift from the nation of Israel and demands an explanation. He asks God to provide an account for the dire events, but God remains silent.

Hello? Anybody home?

In desperation, Habakkuk treads to the front of the city and squats down on his haunches. He waits until God shows up.

Waiting on what comes next often mutates to wondering if there will be a next. In these are the moments, we speculate if we will ever experience:

the miracle of pregnancy.

relief from the pain.

a confirmed healing.

the lawsuit to be finalized.

the long-awaited apology.

Depending on how long we're forced to stay in-between, we can begin to lose hope that we'll ever break free or break through.

In Habakkuk's story, God appears and answers his questions. The prophet bursts forth with hope: "The Lord God is my strength, and He has made my feet like hinds' feet, and makes me walk on my high places" (Habakkuk 3:19 NASB).

Like a sculptor, God shapes us while we wait. Like a teacher, God instructs us while we wait. Like a counselor, God settles us while we wait.

If we believe God is everywhere at any time, then we must accept that God waits with us in the in-between times. We are never alone.

 God does not ask us to wait alone, but rather wait on him alone.

For me and many of my friends who have experienced life-threatening illnesses, the results of the next scan or blood test throw us into extreme anxiety. Time slows as we wait for the images or numbers to return from the medical office.

Sometimes in those moments it's hard to remember that while we wait, God works.

Consider this powerful promise from God: "Those who hope in the LORD will renew their strength. They will soar on wings like eagles; they will run and not grow weary, they will walk and not be faint" (Isaiah 40:31).

God invites restless souls, like my own, to find respite in him. Not only does he listen to our heart's cries as we wait, but he blesses us, strengthens us, and renews our hope in the process.

In the in-between times, God invites us to place the weight of the wait on him. Christ will come again.

FLOURISH TODAY: Make a list of three specific things you're waiting on God for today. Ask God to reveal his faithfulness to you in the in-between.

THIS WEEK'S PRAYER: *Father, Give me grace for the in-between times. Amen.*

Week 36
A MUCH-NEEDED
STUMP SPEECH

I learned one of the most meaningful spiritual lessons of my life in a barn. During a visit with a friend on her farm, I asked why the geese in the barn marched in circles as if searching for something lost.

"They're looking for their eggs," she said.

"Where are they?" I asked.

"I threw them in the creek," she said.

My head cocked to the side, begging for explanation. My friend's actions seemed cold and cruel, a far cry from the woman who tended the land with great care.

"Those eggs were infertile and would never hatch," she explained. "I had to throw them away so the geese could return to the life they were meant to live."

How often do we march around dead dreams that were never going to come to fruition or, worse, sit on the empty promises of the enemy that will never yield life?

One of the deep truths about hope is that sometimes our dreams won't come true in the ways we expect or the timetable we desire. Some of our dreams must be stripped away or released in order for us to move forward into the life God has for us.

Job describes this phenomenon when he speaks about a dead, lifeless stump. "At the scent of water it will flourish and put forth sprigs like a plant" (Job 14:9 NASB).

The once-tall tree chopped by someone or something—an intentional, brutal, sudden demise. No care will be given to the stump because of its appearance. While the roots rot and diminish, the soil ceases to nourish.

Yet, Job says, that the scent of water brings new life. A supply from the skies renews hope. Job suggests that deadness only needs a waft of fresh water to experience revival. The whiff of hope is enough to begin sprouting shoots as if it were a new plant.

In this passage, the word used for "flourish" is *parach* meaning "to bud." The new buds reveal the stump's state of growth.

We need Job's stump speech.

When you let go of a dream, you don't have to release hope, too.

 You don't have to strain when you allow God's hope to sustain.

The tree does not make way for a bench, a pool, or a field of flowers. The tree itself comes to life.

The only thing required for new growth to occur is the presence of water. We have access to the Living Water in Jesus. When a dream dies, we can still sprout hope through Christ.

Flourishing isn't just sustenance and maintenance—it's ever expanding toward a productive and reproductive life.

Sometimes we have to toss away what hinders life or, worse, it is stripped away. But even that gives us hope. Like those pacing geese, we're being moved toward the life God intends.

FLOURISH TODAY: Write down one dream you need to let go of so a new dream budding with hope can grow within you.

THIS WEEK'S PRAYER: *Father, Help me to let go of infertile dreams so I can bud with new hope. Amen.*

Pray & Reflect

At the scent of water it will flourish
and put forth sprigs like a plant.

JOB 14:9 NASB

Blossoming in Freedom

Week 37

WHERE FORGIVENESS GOES

Have you ever heard the expression, "I was so angry that you could've fried an egg on my head"? Well, the other night, I became so mad at Leif I could have opened an omelet bar.

We were driving home when the car in front of us started cruising twenty miles per hour below the speed limit in the fast lane. The vehicle refused to drift into the slow lane.

Leif flashed his lights.

Nothing changed.

He flashed his lights again.

The driver slowed down. In frustration, Leif moved into the slow lane, stepped on the accelerator and sped past.

At this point, all was well. Nothing more than a momentary highway annoyance. But the driver responded by slamming his foot on the gas and tailgating us. For miles.

Leif moved faster. Slower. Toward the other lane.

Wherever we moved, the car followed a few feet behind our bumper.

Twenty miles later, the driver still shadowed our bumper.

I'd heard enough stories of dangerous confrontations with angry road-ragers. Scenes of horror flashed through my mind.

Anger overcame me. How did Leif allow this to happen? And with precious Margaret, his sweet and helpless wife in the car?

"Let's drive to the police station," I suggested.

"Let me see if I can shake him," Leif replied.

Leif swerved from the fast lane to the slow placing a semitruck between us and the other driver, then jetted off an exit ramp. Leif apologized for his part in the situation. We lost the other car but my anger lingered.

I'm usually quick to forgive Leif, but not this time. I couldn't let go. The sun descended and ascended on my anger.

By mid-morning, my heart thawed. I knew I needed to forgive. Leif had not done something unspeakable. *I* had.

I had refused to forgive.

Unforgiveness casts dark shadows on the soul and prevents us from flourishing.

One of my heroes, Frederick Buechner, captures this eloquently when he writes in *Wishful Thinking*:

"To forgive somebody is to say one way or another, 'You have done something unspeakable, and by all rights I should call it quits between us. Both my pride and my principles demand no less. However, although I make no guarantees that I will be able to forget what you've done, and though we may both carry the scars for life, I refuse to let it stand between us. I still want you for my friend.'"[23]

Buechner explains that accepting forgiveness means admitting you've done something "unspeakable." You need to be forgiven. Both parties must swallow their pride.

"When somebody you've wronged forgives you, you're spared the dull and self-diminishing throb of a guilty conscience," he writes. "When you forgive somebody who has wronged you, you're spared the dismal corrosion of bitterness and wounded pride."[24]

 Where forgiveness goes, freedom flows.

When we hold a grudge or cling to animosity, we become shackled to spite and resentment. The only way to dissolve these toxins is through forgiveness.

As the apostle Paul writes, "Be kind and compassionate to one another, forgiving each other, just as in Christ God forgave you" (Ephesians 4:32).

Forgiving and being forgiven are intimately intertwined. If you want to flourish in your relationship with God, you must choose to forgive.

Jesus challenges us: "For if you forgive other people when they sin against you, your heavenly Father will also forgive you. But if you do not forgive others their sins, your Father will not forgive your sins" (Matthew 6:14-15).

If we harbor accusations in our hearts toward others, we're not in a place to accept forgiveness from God. Our forgiveness hinges on forgiving others. We cease to be a conduit of God's mercy and grace whenever we build a wall of unforgiveness.

Unforgiveness inhibits our growth and prevents us from flourishing. But when we choose to let go, we find freedom. And we set free those who have wronged us as well.

Forgiveness frees us from hidden sins of anger, bitterness, and resentment. This release ushers us into a place where true worship of God may flourish as we radiate the beauty of holiness.

Who do you need to forgive? Where do you need to swallow your pride? And regain your freedom?

When it comes to forgiving, don't hit the brakes. Speed up the process and offer it right now.

FLOURISH TODAY: Take the Nike approach with the person you're angriest with: Just do it. Reach out today and let them know all is forgiven.

THIS WEEK'S PRAYER: *Father, Give me the grace to forgive others as you have forgiven me. Amen.*

Week 38
FREE TO LOVE

As an introvert, my friend Tara feels a lava lamp of emotions trapped inside her whenever stuck in a crowd or a one-on-one conversation with a stranger.

"I don't really like people. As terrible as it sounds, it's true," she confesses. "I would do anything for my close knit group of friends, but for the most part, others tend to interrupt my well-organized plans for the day. That annoys me."

Several months ago, Tara woke up early to spend time in her quiet backyard. This space has become a respite of solitude for her, a place where she can breathe deep and recharge. She nested with a coffee, Bible, and a grown-up coloring book filled with Scripture. She inhaled a deep breath.

Thank you, Lord, for blessing me with this opportunity to have my quiet time surrounded by creation, she prayed.

No sooner had she said "amen," then her neighbor appeared outside.

Please, don't let her talk to me, please don't let her talk to me.

Tara tried not to look in her neighbor's direction but she could feel her moving closer. The neighbor reached Tara's yard, greeted her, and showed Tara the fancy garden hose she'd just purchased from QVC.

The neighbor began recounting all its features, the most unique being its ability to expand. When the hose was not being used, the entire coil was no bigger than a cantaloupe.

"But watch this," the neighbor said, hooking it up and turned on the water. The hose grew to more than 50-feet, allowing her to reach new areas of her lawn without effort. Within moments of turning off the water, the hose returned to its original size.

When the neighbor departed, Tara rolled her eyes. Then God stepped in.

"I sensed the Holy Spirit say, '*This is a picture of what you are like when you're not loving others—all coiled up. If you let my love flow through you, look how far you can reach.*'"

What began as an interruption blossomed into a moment of freedom.

Tara discovered the freedom tucked into Jesus' command to love your neighbor. When we open ourselves to water our world with love, God can use us in spectacular, stretching ways. Instead of offering stingy, conditional love, we become mirrors of the way Christ loves us, freeing us to love people without conditions, bounds, or judgment.

Jesus teaches this principle when asked to handpick the greatest commandment.

"'Love the Lord your God with all your heart and with all your soul and with all your mind and with all your strength.' The second is this: 'Love your neighbor as yourself'" (Mark 12:30–31).

When Jesus speaks these words he draws from deep within Leviticus, a book central to the Torah, which lists regulations for priests and laity. At first and even second glance, the hundreds of laws listed in Leviticus appear archaic, difficult to understand. Yet interwoven into these laws are the love-language of God.

Leviticus is God's declaration, "This is how you love me! This is how you walk in greater freedom!"

We expect to find a command to love God here, but Jesus ties five sticks of dynamite around the command words when he adds: love your neighbor *as yourself.*

Jesus knew what would take psychologists many years to discover: The way we treat others reveals how much we love ourselves. The ruthless words we use with others never compares with the barbarous things we say to ourselves. Our interactions, attitudes, and conversations with our neighbors can expose what we really think about ourselves.

Often we don't love others well because we don't love ourselves well. We run ourselves ragged, squirm with resentment, and soak in bitterness because life hasn't turned out the way we hoped. If we refuse goodwill to others, we won't extend it to ourselves.

 When God's love *for* you becomes God's love *in* you, then God's love flows *out* of you.

We must give ourselves permission to love ourselves well. A bubble bath. Our favorite meal. A massage. Extra foam on that latte. Spend time considering all the good gifts God has given you.

You don't have to be an introvert to find wisdom in Jesus' command. These words apply to us when we find ourselves coiled up, easily irritated, or stingy.

Let the living water fill you up and spill out onto others.

FLOURISH TODAY: Do something to take care of yourself today. Treat yourself to something special that you wouldn't normally.

THIS WEEK'S PRAYER: *Father, Set me free to love myself so that I can love others more fully. Amen.*

Week 39
GOODBYE TO GOOD

Someone asked me recently which of the Seven Deadly Sins I struggle with most. I laughed and replied "All of the above" to cover up my inability to recite them.

A little research revealed the Seven Deadly Sins appear in the Bible but not as a single list. These vices have a long snaking history that originates with the desert fathers and takes root in Catholic confessional practices.

The list is woven into many literary works including Dante's *Purgatory*.

Gluttony
Lust
Greed
Pride
Sloth
Wrath
Envy

Glancing over, I wrestled with which sin I struggled with most. My "all of the above" didn't seem like such a joke anymore.

That's because I'm human.

Broken
Imperfect
Hot mess
Conflicted

Human.

Guilt grew as I tangoed with the question of which of the seven sins I wrestled with was my greatest sin.

Then I received some wisdom from my friend, Kate. An accomplished professional and mom to the most adorable, squirmy two-year-old, she lived a vibrant, successful life. But after a routine visit to the doctor she now battles a vicious disease that jeopardizes everything.

Even the smallest moments in Kate's life loom large now. Not a second to waste.

Every moment counts as special.
Every day arrives as a treasure.
Every breath inhales a gift.

"Some days it's too much," she confesses.

Her situation shifts the way she thinks about time, and also the way she reflects on sin:

"The sins—the petty jealousies, the overindulgences, the anger when things don't go my way—those just slough off. They make me laugh. There's no time, no margin, no energy for such silly behavior. The hardest thing to give up isn't letting go of the bad, but letting go of the *good*."

Kate speaks of how hard it is to let go of . . .

one waking moment with her baby girl
one morning in the arms of her husband
one afternoon playing together as a family
one unforgettable holiday party with friends.

As she glows radiant with Christlikeness, she reminds me that as we
journey deeper with God, the challenge shifts from letting go of the
bad to letting go of the good and trusting Christ with all, all, all. This is
crucial to blossoming in freedom.

Perhaps letting go of the good is Jesus' challenge to the sequence of
people in Luke 9 who say they want to follow him but hesitate.

"Lord, first let me go and bury my father," says one (Luke 9:59).

Many Jews considered the supervision of a father's funeral arrangements
a son's chief obligation—greater even than the study of the law or temple
service.

Jesus instructs this son to let the spiritually dead bury their own dead.
Enter real life, an uninhibited life of proclaiming the kingdom of God.

"I will follow you, Lord; but first let me go back and say goodbye to my
family," another says (Luke 9:61).

Again, Jesus exposes the man's reluctance by instructing him not to
return home.

In both cases, sin doesn't tether would-be followers, but much good does. Each of the excuses for not following Jesus is well-meant, culturally justified, and laudable.

 Even the best can distort into something bad when we elevate it above Christ.

How many of us have put our search for a spouse ahead of our relationship with God? How many of us have over-prioritized our kids? How many of us have idolized our jobs?

All good things. All lesser matters when compared to God.

To fully blossom in the freedom of Christ means letting go of the bad *and* the good and following Jesus—

No matter what it costs.
No matter where it leads.
No matter how it ends.

This is a hard won freedom, but one made available to us all through Christ.

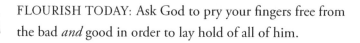

FLOURISH TODAY: Ask God to pry your fingers free from the bad *and* good in order to lay hold of all of him.

THIS WEEK'S PRAYER: *Father, Help me to walk in greater freedom with you each day. Amen.*

I recently heard a story of a woman who had the same, strange vision for forty-five days straight.

In the vision, she watched herself perform a handstand in the middle of a gas station convenience store. No joke.

The first time she experienced the imagery, she brushed it off as a strange dream. Maybe that milk she drank before bed had spoiled. But a month and a half's worth of visions later and she started wondering if maybe God was involved.

Why would God be showing her a vision of a handstand? Was this a metaphor for something? A divine urge to be braver in life?

After the forty-fifth day of the same vision, she was putting gas in her car at a 7-11 filling station. *Maybe God wants me to do a handstand,* she thought.

She peered through the windows and saw no one inside except the cashier. *What is there to lose?*

She walked inside and snuck into a side aisle, hoping the cashier couldn't see her.

Bending down, she placed her hands on the crumb-filled floor, and hoisted up her weight. She did a handstand in the middle of a convenience store, holding the posture for several seconds.

Satisfied that she followed what she thought God might be prompting, she stood up and headed for the door. On her way out, she noticed the cashier crying.

"Did you just do a handstand?" he asked her through sobs.

She nodded.

"Just twenty minutes ago," the cashier continued, "I prayed that if God was real, he would have someone stand on their head in front of me."

The woman knew doing a handstand in a 7-11 seemed risky and absurd, but God used her obedience in ways she couldn't have imagined.

 **You cannot follow God
and stay where you are at the same time.**

To follow God means to live a life littered with risks.

Often God starts small. That gentle nudge to pick up the phone and call a friend or write an encouraging note. As we follow Jesus, we soon discover that the risks he calls us to grow greater, heftier, deeper.

When we respond in risky obedience, we blossom in freedom.

Sometimes following God doesn't look like we expect. The Bible compiles stories of men and women who take great risks for God:

Noah risks zoological mayhem in a boat with animals that eat each other.

Abraham risks a familiar, comfortable life to move into an unknown land.

Moses risks his life to free God's people.

David risks his life with a mad giant and a madman king.

Daniel risks his life in an act of worship.

Ruth risks ever having a good marriage and any descendants to accompany Naomi.

John the Baptist risks imprisonment calling the religious leaders phonies.

Anna risks her senior years waiting for one moment in the temple.

Mary risks her reputation becoming the mother of Jesus.

Ananias risks his life to meet with newly converted Saul.

Paul risks his reputation to become a follower of Christ.

But the story of a Jewish orphan named Esther ranks among the riskiest stories. Her cousin Mordecai who works for the king of Persia and Media raises her. When the king appoints Esther as queen, Mordecai begs her not to reveal her Jewish identity.

Meanwhile, Haman, who also works for the king, hates Mordecai with every fiber of his being and tricks the king into signing a law, a decree that all Jews be killed. When Esther finds out, Mordecai sends her a message asking her to intervene:

"And who knows but that you have come to your royal position for such a time as this?" (Esther 4:14).

Esther, persuaded by Mordecai, appears unannounced before the king, an act punishable by death. The king extends mercy to her, and when Esther later begs for the lives of her people, he grants it. The king instead condemns Haman to death.

God places you where you are for a purpose. If you feel a God-nudge to take a risk, don't brush it aside. Perhaps you've been handpicked to play an outrageous part in God's outstanding plan. Go ahead. Embark on the God-adventure.

FLOURISH TODAY: With prayer, brainstorm a God-caper with a friend and go on an adventure together.

THIS WEEK'S PRAYER: *Father, Set me free from everything that holds me back from risking and following you. Amen.*

Pray & Reflect

If the Son sets you *free,* you will be *free* indeed.

JOHN 8:36

Ripening
with
Resilience

Week 41

THE SOURCE OF RENEWAL

Sitting in the counselor's office after months of cancer treatments,
I felt exasperated by the loss of strength, energy, clarity, sanity. As soon
as I finished one treatment, I entered another. Chemotherapy. Radiation.
More and more surgeries.

Tears flowed down my cheeks as I vented my doubts and frustrations.
Finally, I finished. The counselor paused for a moment, handed me
a box of tissues, and then slapped me across the face with taut words:

"Resilience can run dry."

The statement caught me off guard. I've always thought of resilience
as endless. If you are resilient, the spring *always* bounces back and the
well *always* renews.

The counselor explained wells run dry if enough water is removed.

Thirty years of counseling experience, and he'd seen people like me again
and again. People living like gravity didn't apply, as if they didn't have
boundaries, soon found themselves emptied of resilience, using up their
reserves.

Hollow.
Lifeless.
Former shadows of themselves.

How could I rise again? How could I increase in resilience after I'd been left depleted?

My counselor taught me that rising with resilience meant recognizing my finiteness, including limited resources and energy. I had to give my mind, body, and spirit time to rest and renew. Such self-care is not selfish but good stewardship.

Sprouting with resilience meant discovering the restorative power of a long afternoon nap, an evening walk during sunset, a freshly chopped salad. Simple activities like bubble baths, arranging a fresh bouquet of wild flowers, and playing bocce ball in the backyard with friends began percolating life inside me.

Growing with resilience required a shift in my mindset. I had to extend more grace to myself for what I could do in any given day as well as what I needed to leave undone. Though dirty laundry and dishes piled high, I began sensing a deeper trust of Jesus' ability to heal from the inside out.

A good illustration of this surfaces in the Gospel of Matthew when a leper kneels before Jesus:

"Lord, if you are willing, you can make me clean," he offers (Matthew 8:2).

The man places twin beliefs in Christ—that he is *willing* and he is *able*. Jesus responds by extending healing.

Throughout Matthew 8–9, we discover time and time again that Jesus is

213

willing and able,
willing and able,
willing and able,
willing and able,
willing and able,
willing and able.

Matthew doesn't provide a tally of all who were restored. Instead, he reveals that the One who "took up our infirmities and bore our diseases" is willing and able.

Jesus reveals his power to heal:

the man with leprosy.
a paralyzed servant.
Peter's mother-in-law.
many who were demon possessed.
the ongoing bleeder.
the synagogue leader.
two blind men.

 Jesus is a serial healer.

Never deterred by a ragged list of infirmities, Jesus drips with healing to those in need of refreshment.

But Jesus' power extends beyond healing. Jesus holds the power to calm, the power to redeem, the power to unite, the power to transform, the power to save.

Jesus reveals his power over disorder when he speaks calm over a chaotic sea.

Jesus exposes his power to redeem when he calls a corrupt tax collector to follow him.

Jesus unleashes his power to unite when he invites the exploiters and exploited to feast with him.

I don't know what you've been walking through or what you're facing, but I do know that Jesus possesses the desire and ability to work for your good and God's glory. Jesus is the source of your renewal, the fount of being able to live loved, live fearless, and live free.

Several years after meeting with the counselor, I'm still learning to grow in resilience. I'm still cultivating ways to nurture deep rest and renewal with Christ.

Ripening with resilience doesn't mean that you won't lose some of your bounce. Jesus remains able and willing to work in your life whether you feel empty or full, challenged or charged, weak or strong. Today, you can lean into a Savior who is the source of your eternal resilience.

FLOURISH TODAY: Color the artwork at the end of this section and cut it out and place it in your house to remind you that "God is willing and able."

THIS WEEK'S PRAYER: *Father, I believe you are willing and able to work in my life no matter the circumstances I'm facing. Amen.*

Week 42

THE GREAT PHYSICIAN'S PRESCRIPTION

Have you ever developed a skin irritation and jumped online to try to determine the cause? Before you know it, the faint pink spot on your skin has an unpronounceable name with a prognosis of a swift, painful death.

A visit to Dr. Google's office never goes well.

Because we live in a digital age, we have access to more medical information than ever before. And because we live in a sensational age, stories of terrible and rare diseases abound. As a result, we tend to assume that any hint of a medical problem will lead to the worst diagnosis and will require the most intense medical care.

Often, that skin irritation just needed some over-the-counter hydrating cream for relief. But that doesn't stop us from visiting Dr. Google the next time we find something bothersome.

Tucked into the Old Testament is the story of a rugged prophet and a sick man neither of whom had access to Dr. Google. But they did have access to God.

An army commander, Naaman, asks Elisha to heal him of a skin disease. Elisha sends a servant to tell Naaman to wash in the river. The stubborn soldier refuses and stomps off, mad as a hornet.

Naaman's servants catch up with him and ask, "If the prophet had asked you to do something hard and heroic, wouldn't you have done it? So why not this simple 'wash and be clean'?" (2 Kings 5:13 MSG).

The servant's words pierce the soldier's heart. Naaman recognizes his foolishness. He scrubs himself as Elisha commanded, and the skin disease vanishes.

A valuable lesson is buried in this strange story. Our problems feel huge—they are *our* problems, after all—so we assume the solution should be equally large. We sweep aside any suggestion to the contrary.

In our quests for restoration and healing, many of us spend a lifetime waiting to do the "hard and heroic."

Naaman's story, however, grounds us in the truth:

 God doesn't just work through the hard and heroic but also the simple and steadfast.

We assume the way through our problems will be long and hard. God often waits for us in the simplest solutions that we're tempted to overlook:

The quick phone call with a friend.
The search for a support group.
The words "I love you."
The confession of struggle.
The request for help.

Leaning into the simple ways God wants to work in our lives requires us to be eager learners, trainable, teachable. We must learn to lay aside the need to be in charge.

For several years I've been praying for physical healing. I continue to ask God to heal, and pray that in one moment all will be fully restored.

But laying hold of physical healing requires me to engage in mundane doctor-prescribed regimens. Stretch throughout the day. Don't sit at a computer for more than 20 minutes. Walk 10,000 steps daily. Lift light weights. Attend physical therapy. Eat nutrient-dense foods.

Sometimes these acts feel so basic, I wonder if there's any progress at all. But coupled with prayer, Bible study, and the encouragement of believers, I'm discovering healing taking place—not just in my body, but my heart and mind, too. My strength is returning. Restoration is taking place.

What are the mundane ways God is asking you to pursue restoration?

Look for opportunities to practice the simple and steadfast today.

FLOURISH TODAY: Make a list of what needs healing in your life and the lives of those you love. Take these concerns to the Great Physician in prayer. Respond to any prompts to take action.

THIS WEEK'S PRAYER: *Father, Lead me in the way of healing and wholeness. Amen.*

Week 43
A HELPER IN HEALING

When battling cancer, I noticed a pattern tucked into Jesus' healing stories in Matthew 8–9. A few people *seek* Jesus for their healing, but most are *brought* to Jesus by their friends.

The centurion petitions for his servant.

Among the crowds, "many were brought to him," perhaps because they couldn't bring themselves.

Two demon-possessed men tear across a cemetery to meet Jesus.
Note that they come together.

Two blind men petition for their healing.
Again, note they don't come alone.

Friends carry a paralyzed man to Jesus.

Matthew invites his friends to a banquet with Jesus.

The synagogue leader pleads for his daughter.

In Matthew 8–9, the only people who appear and ask for their healing alone are the man with leprosy and the woman with the issue of blood. *Oh, and Jesus heals them, too.*

Do you recognize the prominent role *friends* play in healing?

Or rather . . .

Do you recognize the role *you* play in the healing of your *friends*?

You and I have people, now, here, today, that we need to bring to Jesus for healing.

We bring them to Jesus through our prayers and petitions.

We bring them to Jesus when we courageously ask, "Would you mind if I pray for you now?"

We bring them to Jesus when we give them the gift of our presence. When we pick up the phone, write the email, send the text, and say, "Tell me what you need."

 Jesus works the miracles, but we can help others heal.

People feel the power of your prayers. Some days, they climb higher, other days they don't sink as low because of the power of prayer.

In my life, knowing that people were praying provided a kind of spiritual buoyancy, steadying me in the midst of great tumult.

Indeed, you, my friend, help bring healing.

Rarely in the church are we taught how to enter people's pain in a way that does no harm and only strengthens resilience and brings healing. We don't know what to say. We don't know what to do.

As a result, we perch on the periphery as those we know and love—old friends and new acquaintances—suffer in pain. We become like the religious leaders who pass by the man beaten and bloody on the side of the road.

But what the good Samaritan and all these men and women healed in Scripture remind us is that we are meant to break the silence and cross the road.

Jesus is waiting with healing in his wings.

Are you ready to take flight?

FLOURISH TODAY: Pick up the phone and call someone who is suffering. Ask what you can do. Then offer three ideas on how you and some friends can serve them.

THIS WEEK'S PRAYER: *Father, show me the friends I need to bring to you for healing, and give me the courage to reach out and rally others on their behalf. Amen.*

Week 44
THE GIFT OF YOU

Over the past few years, I've had well-meaning people speak life, hope, and love into me during the some of the darkest days of battling cancer. Their encouragements were like golden-ripe honey crisp apples served on silver platters (Proverbs 25:11 Margaret Revised Standard Version).

Other times, however, I encountered words that people *intended* to breathe life but hurt instead. These individuals never meant harm, but their words punched me in the gut, leaving me breathless. People mean well, but their words felt mean and didn't leave me feeling well.

Pat answers.
Scriptures ripped out of context.

No, you don't "know exactly how I feel" because your dog had cancer. And I'm sure that açaí berries healed your grandmother's gout, but I need an actual doctor.

Some of the least helpful words came in the form of greeting cards. They read, "In sympathy," and "I'm sorry for your loss." The handwritten words inside breathed life, but many of the store-bought cards felt out of place, penned for those who had loved ones die rather than those who were in an ongoing fight for their lives.

In the stores, I browsed through greeting card aisles. Few to none of the cards were crafted for people with ongoing crisis, loss, or adversity. Those available were *womp womp*.

One day, I will create some cards that will breathe life and hope and love, I pledged.

After more than a year of treatment, I woke up at 2:00 a.m. with an idea to create greeting cards for people who don't know what to say. Six month later, I worked with a designer to create a line of Do No Harm cards that encourage people with messages including:

I can't imagine all you're facing but know the rest of us live in wonder and awe of you.

In case no one has told you today, you are strong, you are brave, you are amazing us all.[25]

I've heard from so many who say that these cards have served as a passport to help them reenter friends' lives after times of tragedy. They provide a means to reconnect and rejuvenate bonds of friendship.

I love that.

But I remind people that a card is never enough. Even the most encouraging words never substitute for face-time with a friend.

If you want to sprout resilience in others, offer the gift of your ongoing presence.

Jesus reveals the importance of this on the evening he invites his three closest wingmen—Peter, James, and John—to join his prayer posse in the Garden of Gethsemane.

Perhaps Peter hoped he'd catch a glimpse of another transfiguration of Jesus on the rocky mountain top. If he had one, Peter might have slipped his cell phone in his back pocket, ready for some epic selfie. But instead, the trio witnesses a different transformation. Jesus' expression morphs before their eyes.

The countenance of the one they adore darkens. With furrowed brows and a tightened jaw, Jesus confesses, "My soul is overwhelmed with sorrow to the point of death" (Mark 14:34).

Then Jesus makes a startling request, "Stay here and keep watch with me" (v. 34).

The disciples are confused by the day's events, their bodies exhausted from travel. Jesus' groans and cries soon fade as they nod off to sleep despite Jesus' plea for them to stay awake and spend time with him.

He wakes them, but his friends, his besties, doze again. They're asleep to what he has asked of them.

This time, of all times, Jesus desires his closest disciples with him. He could have gone to Gethsemane alone. He'd climbed countless other hills by himself.

Yet this night.
This one night.
He wants his friends with him—awake, alert, praying.

They miss his request for presence. And we do, too.

224

Discoveries of sickness, death, divorce, custody battles, abuse, affairs, and addiction scare us. When we don't understand life's events—whether a breakup or a mysterious illness—we're tempted to withdraw.

The list of excuses for extracting ourselves runs long. We don't want to bother. We don't think we have the strength to see them that way. We don't know the words to speak or the actions to take. Or, like the disciples, we're tired.

When we remain silent toward those in need, we don't live loved, live fearless, or live free. But when we answer Jesus' invitation to stay alert and awake to the needs of others, we serve a crucial role in helping them flourish.

When you step into the presence of suffering, you stumble into the presence of God.

Remember that you carry Christ inside of you.

The gift of your presence requires you to be brave. Be available. Listen. Love. Laugh. Exhale the Jesus-life inside you.

FLOURISH TODAY: Pick one person and reach out. Offer no advice, no judgment. Simply be with them.

THIS WEEK'S PRAYER: *Father, Help me to give the gift of my presence to others as freely as you offer me the gift of yours. Amen.*

Pray & Reflect

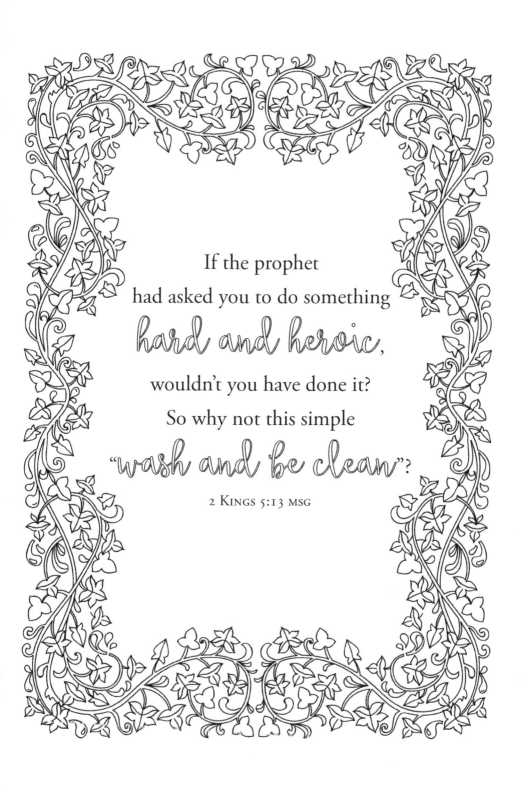

If the prophet
had asked you to do something
hard and heroic,
wouldn't you have done it?
So why not this simple
"wash and be clean"?

2 KINGS 5:13 MSG

Bursting
with Life

Week 45

WORD POWER

I'll never forget the day I came to understand words' life-giving power.

I was asked to speak at a national women's event that featured popular Bible teachers such as Jennie Allen, Ann Voskamp, and Shelley Giglio. *Had someone mailed the invitation to the wrong address?* I accepted in a flash before anyone noticed the error.

Never one to pass up a golden opportunity, I imbibed the wisdom that was shared by the amazing lineup of teachers and authors, every chance I had. Rather than sit backstage in the speaker's lounge, I slipped into the audience.

I was like a blade of grass soaking up the high-noon sun.

The talks and interviews inspired me, yet the words pinned in my heart came from a woman whose name I may never know. A person I'd never met before. A face that's still a mystery to me.

The program concluded. The attendees emptied out. The stage dismantled. The chairs stacked and carried away.

As I walked toward the exit, a woman approached me, her aged, delicate countenance brimmed with wisdom and grace. I suspected she'd been in ministry for many years. On staff at a church? A pastor's wife? A mom who'd spent decades tenderly rearing her kids?

I did not know.

Her stride was confident, and her eyes locked on me. She acknowledged that she had heard me speak then grabbed my elbow, stared with the most compassionate, penetrating eyes, and declared:

"I have only one thing to say to you: Stay in the game."

She turned, then walked away. Time froze. I stood breathless. Her words hung in the air.

The four words from that conference that danced in my mind and heart months later didn't come from a well-polished speaker or a famed author. They came from a stranger.

Stay in the game.

I shouldn't be surprised that a few syllables have the potential to transform my life. The ancient king, Solomon, had whispered this truth to me many times before:

"The mouth of the righteous is a fountain of *life*" (Proverbs 10:11).

"Gentle words are a tree of *life*" (Proverbs 15:4 NLT).

"The tongue has the power of *life* and death, and those who love it will eat its fruit" (Proverbs 18:21).

Like seeds planted deep in the ground, that grow and change the entire landscape, the Bible connects the words we use with life itself.

**The syllables you speak
nourish life or dispense death.**

Some days we feel…

overtaxed and overmaxed.

worn down and beat up.

irritated by others.

underappreciated by our boss.

unloved by our significant other.

drained by responsibility.

On these days we need words that help us flourish as much as we need our next breath. We can't control what other people say to us, and we definitely don't want to fish for compliments. But we can pray for God to send someone to speak life to us.

The difficult days provide opportunities for us to remember that we aren't the only ones who struggle:

The server who doesn't pay you enough attention may be a hard-pressed single mom.

The small group teacher whose lesson fell flat may be doing everything they can to hold their marriage together.

And the IRS auditor, well, he's just doing his job to provide for his family.

What if you began speaking the words to others that you need on your worst days?

Words don't just affect individuals, they impact communities. When you recognize the gravity of your words, you're more likely to stop and give consideration to how and when you use them.

Wherever you find yourself right now, people in your life need the life that your words can bring. Others need you to stop killing them with your comments. Some days you'll steward your words well; other days you'll fail. But never forget that what you say matters more than you know.

FLOURISH TODAY: Call a friend and challenge yourself to speak words of life to them for five minutes straight. This sounds like a paltry amount of time, but don't be fooled. Prepare yourself to be challenged.

THIS WEEK'S PRAYER: *Father, May my words be a fountain of life for someone else today and may someone else's words become water for my parched roots. Amen.*

TIME FOR AN EYE EXAM

Some time ago, I enrolled in a class to become a certified lifeguard.
The instructor moved through the material at a snail's pace, and
I thought we'd never make it through the week's course material.
I judged the young teacher as unskilled and unprepared for the
lessons, and my perspective began affecting my words.

In a flash I became her judge, and I ruled her unfit for the job.

I muttered under my breath whenever she repeated herself. I surveyed
the other students during breaks to make sure I wasn't the only one.
I bemoaned her abilities to Leif at night.

I soon noticed that I dreaded attending class. I couldn't stand sitting
in my chair or even seeing the instructor's face. Classmates began
avoiding me at the snack machine. I even suspected Leif was sneaking
in ear plugs so he'd doze off before I could vent to him. My words had
soured us all.

During the final day's lunch break, the young teacher began to share
about her life. While walking in downtown Denver, a car barreled
through the crosswalk and struck her in a hit and run. Over the previous
two years, she relearned to do what doctors declared impossible:
speaking and walking again.

Teaching the class exhausted her, but she loved every moment. If she
could endure the week, one day she might be able to hold a full-time job.

My heart burned like a branding iron that seared "love thy neighbor" in my chest.

"Why do you look at the speck of sawdust in your brother's eye and pay no attention to the plank in your own eye? How can you say to your brother, 'Let me take the speck out of your eye,' when all the time there is a plank in your own eye?" Jesus asks in Matthew 7:3–4.

To illustrate the absurdity and dangers of judging others, Jesus leans into rabbinic hyperbole when he asks the above questions. He paints a comic portrait from a carpenter's workshop that exposes our hypocrisy.

Remove the tree trunk from your eye first, then your vision will be restored so you can extract the sawdust from someone else. Judgment distorts and exaggerates our vision like funhouse mirrors and exposes a habit that affects us all:

 Focusing on others' flaws blinds us to our own.

Jesus could have used any imagery including a splinter in the finger versus a stake through the palm, but he chose to zero in on our inability to see clearly.

Within the Hebraic context, "eye" was used as a common idiom to describe a person's attitude toward others. To have a "good eye" or *ayin tovah* describes someone who is generous and open-hearted. Free of envy or greed, a person with a good eye lives on high alert for ways to meet the needs of others and serve the poor. Those with *ayin tovah* are satisfied with their lot in life and quick to celebrate the success of others.

The primary lenses through which life is viewed with *ayin tovah* are love and generosity. The good eye looks at everyone and everything in search of something beautiful or blessed, seeks out the person's value and virtue. The good eye stands in sharp contrast to the bad eye, *ayin hara*. The bad eye is hasty to judge, full of mistrust, and seeks the company of darkness. It sees others as a threat, inverts values, and heralds the insignificant over the eternal.

Why is a person's "eye" so important to Jesus?

Because a good eye helps us see people as Christ sees them and empowers us to love as Christ loves. For me, the lifeguard instructor became a source of inspiration and a hero. With a good eye, I could recognize the restoration taking place in her life.

But a good or bad eye doesn't just affect the way we see others, but the way we see God. We can look at God with love and generosity, trusting him at every turn, or if we're not careful we can view God through the lens of judgment and fear, blinding us to the one true source of light.

Jesus' command to stop judging invites us to live free and view the world anew. Because the way we perceive with our eyes determines the words we speak with our mouths.

FLOURISH TODAY: Identify your nemesis. Name and record their five best qualities.

THIS WEEK'S PRAYER: *Father, Help me to develop a good eye to see others as you do. Amen.*

Week 47
HOW TO (NOT) ENJOY LIFE

As we sat around our wooden barnyard door table in the living room, my friends Jonathan and Carolyn shared the details of their recent trip to a remote monastery in New Mexico.

Jonathan had decided to take a three-day vow of silence at the hermitage. During the span, he didn't say a word, which turned out to be far more of a challenge than expected.

While other pilgrims were free to talk, he wore a wooden pendant around his neck as a sign to others of the vow he'd taken. Everyone noticed and left him alone except for one older, friendly monk, who seemed to ignore the pendant and chat at Jonathan every free moment.

Jonathan learned to nod and shrug and make hand signals, like a befuddled mime, engaging in a full conversation without ever saying a word.

"It was like playing charades with someone for three whole days," Carolyn laughed.

The primitive living conditions were winceworthy. Makeshift wooden cabins leaked icy air throughout the night. The lumpy, hard mattress smelled a hundred years old. The shower lacked a water heater. Meals were consumed in silence; the food cooked without spice and eaten quickly. A snake scared the heebie-jeebies out of them late one night.

My side ached from laughing as they recounted all the kooky details.

"That's way too rustic for me!" I said. "No way I'd last!"

"Carolyn, did you notice that none of it was that bad until I finished
the vow of silence this morning?" Jonathan asked.

The moment he could use his voice, he mentioned the cold showers and
the water became icier. As soon as he complained about breakfast, the
food became more tasteless. Within a few minutes of moaning about
the hardness of the chapel benches, his back and neck began to ache.
Nothing was that bad until he spoke the words aloud.

The conversation danced late into the evening, but Jonathan's
observation haunted me long after they left. Our words contain more
power than we realize.

Voicing complaints aggravates a situation.

With such high stakes, no wonder the apostle Paul draws such hard
lines: "Do everything without complaining and arguing" (Philippians
2:14 NLT). No room for loopholes here. The root Greek word for
"complaining" is *goggysmos* and denotes the idea of secret displeasure,
begrudging attitude, or fussy discontent.

Paul knows the temptation to gripe as well as anyone. Over the course
of his life, he endures false accusations, brutal beatings, wrongful
imprisonment, shipwrecks, and a near drowning. His message is rejected.

His churches fail. His friends turn on him. Paul has endless reasons to complain, but learns the power of holding his tongue and instructs the Philippians to do not just *some* but *all* things without complaint.

Paul never suggests that believers deny any sorrow or adversity they face, but rather recognize, that even in the midst of affliction, they can control their tongue—including the brash and sass.

This self-discipline doesn't just ward off disputes and feuds, but allows us to walk in greater holiness and contentment and so demonstrate to others the distinction that comes with being a child of God.

 **Today's complaints
never make for a better tomorrow.**

Paul purports that something wildly transformative happens when we hold our tongue. In what sometimes feels like nothing more than stuffy, dead air, or awkward silence, the light and life of Christ are being unleashed.

When we choose to respond ready and cheerful, we become like a breath of fresh air in a smog-choked city. Those around us catch snapshots of God, and we see the world in a better light.

Voicing complaints sharpens life's edges and increases pain. Setting a goal of never, ever, ever complaining may seem unrealistic, but pays off big time. Start now.

FLOURISH TODAY: Give permission to the person you spend the most time with to change the subject or interrupt you when you complain.

THIS WEEK'S PRAYER: *Father, May my complaints be few so my joy can be multiplied. Amen.*

Week 48

WHEN WORDS
COME BACK TO HURT

Where did all this negativity come from? My Jewish grandmother was the first who taught me how to *kvetch*, the Yiddish word for "grumble." She turned complaining into a sport. If I introduced her to the most perfect boyfriend, meal, or outfit, she'd give voice to a hidden facet of imperfection.

While her attention to detail sharpened my editorial skills, taught me to ask quirky questions, and made me a savvier shopper (always check the can for dents before you buy), it's ruined me for noticing all of the splotches, cracks, and scuffs in life, other people, and myself.

Without realizing, Grandma taught me that if you examine anything long enough, a deficiency will emerge, and such a deficit should be discussed.

For years, my critical spirit went unchecked. I created a loophole by calling my negativity "snarkiness." Being snarky, or offering satirical witticisms in the form of snide remarks, provides the perfect format for hiding sarcasm, cynicism, or complaint in broad daylight. Plus, the Bible doesn't technically say anything about being snarky, though perhaps Eugene Peterson might phrase Philippians 2:14, "Do everything without snark or spite," if he penned the passage today.

While the Bible may not use the word "snark," both testaments speak about criticism. In the Gospel of Matthew, Jesus says, "Do not judge, or you too will be judged. For in the same way you judge others, you will be judged, and with the measure you use, it will be measured to you" (Matthew 7:1-2).

Jesus warns that criticism hurts you as much as others. The critical spirit boomerangs. Whenever we jump on others' stumbles and snafus, we soon become the center of scrutiny.

 Those who toss crumbs of criticism are soon eaten alive.

Criticism is not always verbal either. Just because you don't *say* anything doesn't mean you aren't critical. Your eyes, arms, and hips can criticize just like your groans, words, and lips.

When a trip overseas required some vaccinations, I sat in the waiting room alongside Leif. With a busy day ahead of us, I encouraged Leif that we get in and out of the appointment fast.

A nurse greeted us and led us down a narrow hallway to her office. She peppered us with questions about where exactly we were traveling, the duration of our visit and the extent of our activities. After a few moments, she slipped out to secure the shots.

"She's not very friendly," I said, realizing a complaint had escaped my lips.

"It's not just her," Leif replied.

"What do you mean?" I asked.

"Look at the way you're sitting," he said. "You look like this!"

He crossed his arms curtly, face hardened, lips drawn tight.

His somber mime exposed that I'd been complaining from the moment I arrived without ever uttering a syllable. I didn't want to go to the doctor's office to be poked by needles—who does? —and I longed to be anywhere that didn't involve hearing someone count down 3-2-1 before she inflicted a piercing, burning oww-ie. I had mastered the art of complaining without a peep.

If you're like me, your critical spirit comes out in some mixture of verbal and nonverbal language triggered by even the smallest inconveniences, obstacles, and annoyances.

We gripe about the bothersome nature of work deadlines, the late payment of a client, the leaky kitchen faucet, the bathroom floor that feels like a sandy beach on our bare feet.

When our favorite jeans no longer fit, we huff. When the neighbors' dog barks all night, we shoot them a dirty look across the street. When that maniac cuts us off in traffic, we lay on our car horn.

Often these behaviors make their way back to us.

God wants to expose the places where we are prone to fuss through our words, postures, and actions. In turn, we can offer attitudes that burst with love and grace, that invite us and others to live free from the judgment of others.

Life is sweeter without criticism. No matter what your grandmother says.

FLOURISH TODAY: During three separate conversations this week, focus on doing these actions: (1) unfold your arms, (2) nod approvingly, (3) keep a constant smile.

THIS WEEK'S PRAYER: *Father, Help me to burst with life this week through both my words and my actions. Amen.*

Pray & Reflect

Gentle words are a tree of life.

PROVERBS 15:4 NLT

Cultivated
by
Christ

Week 49

DEEP AND WIDE

Most people I know grew up in a house. I was raised on a sailboat.

People often have a romantic vision of life at sea. The freedom of setting sail to a new port. The abundance of fresh seafood. The ease of life sans schedule.

But like running a bed and breakfast or starting your own business, life on a boat sounds better than the daily reality.

Boat life overflows with challenges, especially felt at meal times. Fresh lettuce became an impossible-to-find commodity. We created makeshift salads from four-month old cabbage and whatever scraggly vegetable we could find on a remote island off the Florida coast.

During the dry months, we hiked along rustic paths in search of fresh water in hidden cisterns and hauled heavy jugs of it back to the dinghy. Once aboard, we filtered out the baby frogs so they didn't multiply in our water tanks.

We set sail in the early 1980s, before GPS and satellite phones became affordable. My mom guided us with a sextant and compass, sometimes confirming our direction with the stars. "Detours" off course weren't unusual.

When something aboard the boat broke, which seemed like every other day, we were dependent on others to bring replacement parts. If no one was around, we would pray that God would work a miracle with duct tape and a bag of bolts—our version of fishes and loaves.

When you live on a vessel, you have to learn to survive with whatever you possess. You also learn to read the Gospels differently—especially the sea stories and fishing metaphors.

The Gospel of Luke finds Simon employed as a fisherman—an occupation in which an unsuccessful day takes a physical and emotional toll. A sense of defeat surfaces when a fisherman ties up at home empty-handed.

A stranger, Jesus, asks to borrow Simon's boat, not for a fishing expedition, but to use as a floating podium. Simon offers his wooden sea craft.

Jesus balances on the edge of the wooden vessel and teaches the crowd that lines the shore. Upon conclusion, he turns to Simon:

"Put out into deep water, and let down the nets for a catch" (Luke 5:4).

Taking a quick dip at a beach reveals the difference between the shallows and the depths.

The shallows are where your feet touch the bottom, and sand collects in unspeakable parts of your bathing suit. The shallows are where you can convince yourself that if something large and ominous approaches, you can make to shore in time. The shallows feel safe and familiar.

The depths are a place of darkness and uncertainty and risk. A place where waves roll taller than ships, and your feet never touch ground. In the depths, you can't spot land and have to trust the stars.

No wonder Simon waffles a little at Jesus' request: "Master, we've worked hard all night and haven't caught anything. But because you say so, I will let down the nets" (Luke 5:5).

Simon's day job requires him to know the tides, the currents, the wind, the temperature, the best and worst times to catch fish. No wonder when a rabbi instructs a fisherman on what to do, Simon balks at the request.

We can empathize with Simon at this point. Humans are hesitant to plunge into the depths—not just sea, but also in life. We balk at the deep conversation in which we speak our fears aloud. We shy away from deeper involvement in a church community, afraid we may get hurt again. We pause at the thought of committing to another "'til death do us part."

Simon recognizes Jesus teaches like no other. And so, because Jesus, the "Master" asks, the crew uncover their freshly washed nets and venture toward the deep.

No sooner do the nets cascade over the gunwales than they scoop up so many wiggling fish that they begin to split. The boat cannot contain the superabundance.

 God calls us from life's shallow spaces to life's deeper places.

These areas abound with discomfort and risk and messiness and uncertainty. But the depths are also places where...

Jesus meets us.

Jesus provides for us.

Jesus reveals himself to us.

Jesus works miracles.

The call to *the depths* is terrifying. Sea monsters and chaos reside there. But Jesus lingers there, too, inviting us to live fearless. Resist the temptation to hug the shore. Christ waits to fill your nets.

FLOURISH TODAY: Reflect on three areas where you sense Christ beckoning you into the depths. Ask God to lead you there.

THIS WEEK'S PRAYER: *Father, Lead me into the depths of knowing Your power like never before. Amen.*

Week 50
FOXES IN THE HENHOUSE

I've told you I live in the desert. I also reside in a zoo.

Whenever I hike through the rugged mountains of Utah, I stay on high alert. The areas just outside of the developed parts of our city abound with rattlesnakes, mountain lions...

And sometimes a quick-witted fox.

Don't be fooled by these furry creatures' sweet faces. Beneath them lie crafty and conniving, sneaky and shrewd beasts. Foxes love anything shiny or sheeny. Be warned: These cunning thieves will tote your treasures away.

Many years ago, my mom left a family heirloom on her downstairs deck. By morning, the silver bowl had vanished. A determined woman, she spent the following three days searching the surrounding neighborhood and woods.

Nestled in a gulley, she found the foxes' den—where her silver bowl along with a long-lost jacket had been vaulted away.

How intriguing that Jesus refused to let any cunning fox—including Herod—get the best of him.

In Luke 13, some well-intended religious leaders tell Jesus that he better skedaddle. Herod plans to tear Jesus to shreds.

Without wavering, Jesus retorts, "Go tell that fox, 'I will keep on driving out demons and healing people today and tomorrow, and on the third day I will reach my goal'" (Luke 13:32).

Jesus knows his life is in peril so long as he stays in Jerusalem's city limit. How does he behave in response to the threat?

"Jerusalem, Jerusalem, you who kill the prophets and stone those sent to you, how often I have longed to gather your children together, as a hen gathers her chicks under her wings, and you were not willing" (Luke 13:34).

When faced with a cunning fox, Jesus responds with the heart of a hen. He outsmarts and outwits the crafty fox without playing by the fox's rules.

Jesus invites followers.
Herod commands armies.

Jesus gives all that he has.
Herod takes anything he wants.

Jesus displays God's power.
Herod desires to overpower.

Jesus serves.
Herod rules through fear.

Jesus intercedes for his enemies.
Herod squashes those who oppose him.

Jesus is setting up a choice we must all make—not just between foxes and chickens, but also between two ways of being.

 When you grow in gentleness, you glow with godliness.

Jesus' words signal the sadness of one whose divine affection has been snubbed. Jerusalem rejects the motherly protection of a hen's wings. Israel prefers a sly fox for a ruler.

We might judge the Jews for rejecting Jesus, but their choice seems like the best bet. If you were forced to wager, would you gamble on the chicken or the fox?

Yet Jesus outfoxes the fox by becoming a hen—a vulnerable, nurturing creature ready to throw herself between anything or anyone that attacks her loved ones.

A farmer once shared with me how a hen will protect her chicks at all costs. He explained that in the wake of a fire, underneath the charred remnants of a mother hen, the chicks have been found still alive.

Hens lay down their lives for their tender young.

Maybe we shouldn't be surprised that when Jesus sights a fox, he reveals himself as a hen.

As the author Barbara Brown Taylor observes:

"It may have looked like a minor skirmish to those who were there, but that contest between the chicken and the fox turned out to be the cosmic battle of all time, in which the power of tooth and fang was put up against the power of a mother's love for her chicks. And God bet the farm on the hen."[26]

Jesus teaches, by example, that we must resist the temptation to run from foxes or become like them. Rather, we must learn to spread our wings to all of God's children as we live loved and pass that love and security to others. When we are cultivated by Christ, our response will be tamed by loving gentleness.

FLOURISH TODAY: When you're tempted to engage in selfish gain at others' expense, take rather than give or manipulate others through fear, pause instead. Take five seconds and consider a more henlike approach.

THIS WEEK'S PRAYER: *Father, Help me to exchange foxlike actions for henlike responses. Amen.*

Week 51
GOOD RIDDANCE
TO COMPARISONS

Perhaps the most misunderstood story in the New Testament is Mary and Martha's in Luke 10.

While in Bethany, Jesus and the disciples visit these two sisters. Martha, whose name can be translated as "lady," greets her guests with great warmth.

As a capable hostess, she buzzes around the home: picks up loose items, shoos away the stray cat, serves beverages, and prepares the meal. Martha's gifts create an atmosphere where guests feel welcomed and comfortable. Everyone knows it—especially Jesus. On previous visits to one of his favorite families, he likely oohed and aahed over her meals, expressing gratitude for her hard work.

As Martha slices and dices, Mary sits rapt at Jesus' feet.

This position contains significance since Jewish disciples sit at the feet of their chosen rabbis. Jesus welcomes Mary to learn from him just like the other disciples. But Mary isn't the only one who considers Jesus as Lord.

As an affable hostess, Martha becomes distracted or overoccupied by the tasks at hand. Most likely fuming, she calculates the best way to address the rabbi. Perhaps she speaks every... word... extra... slow... in an effort to mask her frustration, or maybe she blurts with great speed.

"Lord, do You not care that my sister has left me to do all the serving alone? Then tell her to help me," she said (Luke 10:40 NASB).

Martha appeals to Jesus to settle the matter.

Jesus recognizes the stress and distress created by the situation.

"Martha, Martha, you are worried and bothered about so many things; but only one is necessary, for Mary has chosen the good part, which shall not be taken away from her" (Luke 10:41–42 NASB).

Martha's desire to flourish had led to a multivolume to-do list. Rather than answer her many concerns, Jesus whispers her name twice in loving gentleness. He knows Martha better than she knows herself; he loves Martha far better than she loves herself.

Ever so tender, Jesus identifies the core issue behind Martha's frustration. It's neither in the chopping of cucumbers nor the unwashed pans.

Martha has become panicky.

Some scholars believe Jesus is referring to the many dishes of food. Martha has overreached in her menu. Others suggest that Martha's unhappiness is a result of a host of activities and duties. Whatever specifics may vex Martha, only Jesus knows.

While some translations suggest Mary favored the "better" part, the original Greek word means "good." Jesus does not pit Martha against Mary nor compare the two sisters. This isn't a rift between the activist life and the contemplative life as some have suggested. Mary has the privilege of listening to the teachings of Jesus, and that is not to be taken from her.

I always read Jesus' words to Martha as a rebuke for becoming distracted and inattentive, but now I see them as a loving invitation.

Tucked in Jesus words is a call to simplify and to slow down. "Only a few things are necessary, really only one."

I always thought Jesus, here, compares Mary to Martha. So often we try to behave like one and not the other. Instead, Jesus doesn't shame either sister, even though we may be tempted to, but he extends an invitation to abide in him.

Do you ever fall victim to the marauder of comparison? Maybe it is with your sibling who still outpaces you at everything? Or perhaps the neighbor who outparents you? Or maybe the pesky friend who outdoes you at almost everything?

 **The comparison trap
beats people down
rather than build them up.**

Jesus never appraises us by how we compare, but according to grace.

When I fully abide in Christ, then I'm not trying to be like Mary or Martha. I naturally resemble the Messiah.

When this is my goal, I'm empowered to quit comparison with others altogether, and I root myself in a liberating truth: What matters is not what I do but what Christ does for and through me.

FLOURISH TODAY: Center on Christ today. Open to any Gospel and read the red words—the words of Jesus—in at least one chapter.

THIS WEEK'S PRAYER: *Father, Thank you for using grace as the measuring stick for my life. Amen.*

Week 52

AN INVITATION TO RESIDE

"Blessed is the one who trusts in the Lord,
    whose confidence is in him.
They will be like a tree planted by the water
    that sends out its roots by the stream.
It does not fear when heat comes;
    its leaves are always green.
It has no worries in a year of drought
    and never fails to bear fruit."
(Jeremiah 17:7–8)

Imagine being a Jew in the first century who had studied this passage from childhood. You know that life as God intends is a loved, free, and fearless existence. The image Jeremiah offers is of a lush tree on the bank of a stream that is bursting with fruit. And then you hear a traveling rabbi draw on another agricultural image:

"I am the vine; you are the branches. If you remain in me and I in you, you will bear much fruit; apart from me you can do nothing" (John 15:5).

We can't know for sure whether Jesus had Jeremiah in mind, but many parallels exist.

But unlike Jesus' metaphor, only one person emerges in Jeremiah's— "the one who trusts in the Lord." Two people appear in Jesus' talk about flourishing like a vine—"I" and "you."

Jesus describes the relationship between these two people with a verb not often used today: abiding. "Reside" or "stay" are the closest synonyms.

 We flourish when we pursue the life God intends.

We must reside in Christ. We must stay with Christ. We must be connected to Christ.

When you're joined to the vine,

the bond creates intimacy.
the harvest yields abundance.
fruitfulness abounds.
you're apt to live loved, live fearless, live free.

Still don't know if you reside in Christ? Jesus drives the point home:

"If you do *not* remain in me, you are like a branch that is thrown away and withers; such branches are picked up, thrown into the fire and burned" (John 15:6).

When you're separated from the vine,

you are deadwood.
you lack life.
you feel disconnected.
you bear no fruit.

Jesus invites us to make our home in him. To move in. Lay the carpet.

Paint the walls. Hang the artwork. Flip on the teakettle. Nestle in the comfy chair. Invite the neighbors over. Reside in him.

The image of abiding brims with rest and peace.

Throughout his earthly ministry, Jesus makes a frequent habit of doling out peace; he might have been mistaken as a child with a Pez candy dispenser. He gives freely to anyone who askes—and even some who don't.

Wander the earth and seek affirmation, love, and peace from anyone or anything else and you will experience stress, frustration, lack of self-worth, and many other side effects. Abide with the Prince of Peace and you will experience joy, love, grace, self-control, and so much more.

Often we choose to chase after the lesser things of this world, like a dog who hopes to one day catch his tail. When God calls us to

Rest.

In.

Christ.

What if you answer the invitation to abide in Christ, to take up residence in him?

Receiving Jesus is not an end, but the means to a greater end. Jesus invites you to a life of loving intimacy with God.

The life of God is fulfilling and fructifying.

You are created to be planted in love, rooted in trust, grounded in wisdom, nourished by community, growing in grace, prepared for drought, protected from floods, budding with hope, blossoming in freedom, ripening with resilience, bursting with life, and cultivated by Christ in such a way that you and those around you thrive.

Flourishing people are joyous, fruitful people who have a positive effect on their community and leave a powerful legacy for the future by modeling the beautiful life of following Jesus.

Together, may we walk in the maturity that allows us to grow deeper, reach farther, and bear more fruit than we ever thought possible because we are his.

FLOURISH TODAY: During your prayer time this week, don't say a word. Sit in silence. Abide and listen.

THIS WEEK'S PRAYER: *Father, Help me abide in you throughout this day. Amen.*

Pray & Reflect

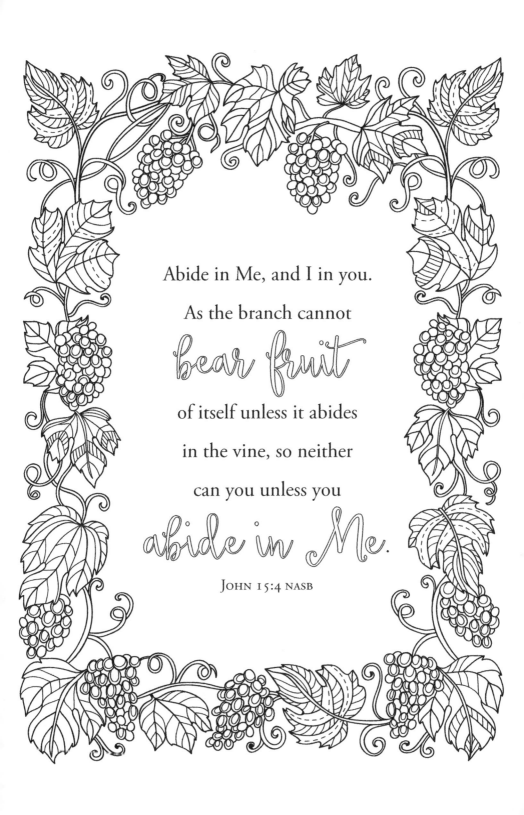

Abide in Me, and I in you.

As the branch cannot

bear fruit

of itself unless it abides

in the vine, so neither

can you unless you

abide in Me.

JOHN 15:4 NASB

NOTES

Note to reader: Names and details have been changed throughout the manuscript to honor privacy.
Any italics in Scripture is added by author for emphasis.

1   Psalm 1:1-3; Isaiah 11:1-3a

2   David L. Bartlett and Barbara Brown Taylor, eds., *Feasting on the Word, Year B* (Louisville, KY: Westminster John Knox Press, 2010), 2:534.

3   Exodus 20:2; Isaiah 41:13; Isaiah 43:1

4   Luke 19:37; 23:13, 18–21

5   Dallas Willard, *The Divine Conspiracy* (New York: Harper, 1998), 349.

6   Thanks to Ellen Charry and her book *God and the Art of Happiness*, (Grand Rapids: Eerdmans, 2010), 216–230 for her insights on wisdom and human flourishing in this section on wisdom.

7   Adapted from "Chasing Woman Wisdom" sermon by Troy Champ, May 28, 2011. Used with permission.

8   Henry Cloud, *Necessary Endings: The Employees, Businesses, and Relationship that All of Us Have to Give Up In Order to Move Forward* (New York: Harper Business, 2010), 119–47.

9   Lois Tverberg, *Walking in the Dust of Rabbi Jesus: How the Jewish Words of Jesus Can Change Your Life* (Grand Rapids, MI: Zondervan, 2012), 34.

10 Tal Ben-Shahar, *Happier: Learn the Secrets to Daily Joy and Lasting Fulfillment.* (New York: McGraw Hill, 2007), 114–15.

11 http://www.goodreads.com/quotes/20318-grace-is-the-most-perplexing-powerful-force-in-the-universe. Emphasis added.

12 https://www.barna.org/faith-spirituality/619-are-christians-more-like-jesus-or-more-like-the-pharisees#.Vor3Rjb6fNU

13 Ibid.

14 John the Baptist's clothing is also tied to his role of being the "Elijah" who heralded the coming Messiah. John dresses like Elijah.

NOTES

15   Highly recommend the following: Alicia Britt Chloe, *Anonymous: Jesus' Hidden Years . . . and Yours* (Nashville: Integrity Publishers, 2006), 142.

16   Exodus 12:31–36

17   Peter Enns, *Exodus: The New Application Commentary* (Grand Rapids, MI: Zondervan, 2000), 273.

18   Exodus 15

19   Claudia Wallis, *The Multitasking Generation*. Time Magazine, March 27, 2006.

20   http://www.theatlantic.com/health/archive/2013/01/
     study-if-you-multitask-often-youre-impulsive-and-bad-at-multitasking/272485/

21   https://medium.com/@hughmcguire/why-can-t-we-read-anymore-503c38c131fe

22   Jessicataylordesign.com

23   Frederick Buechner, *Wishful Thinking: A Theological ABC* (New York: Harper and Row, 1993), 28–29.

24   Ibid.

25   You can see the full line of "What to Say When You Don't Know What to Say" greeting cards at www.margaretfeinbergstore.com

26   This post inspired and written with much gratitude from "Foxes and Chickens". Barbara Brown Taylor, *Bread of Angels* (Plymouth, UK: Rowman and Littlefield, 1997), 129.

270

ACKNOWLEDGMENTS

Thank you to so many who have helped Leif and me begin
flourishing again.

Thank you to Jonathan Merritt, my writing buddy, who came to Salt
Lake City and dreamed up this project in the same kids' Sunday-school
classroom as *Wonderstruck*. Beep. Beep. Boop. I couldn't have done this
without you.

Thank you to Craig Blomberg, Tracee Hackel, Debra Anderson, Kate
Bowler, and Jessica Richie for their insightful comments and feedback.
You made this book so much better and taught me the difference
between waiver and waver for which I will never waver, I think.

ABOUT THE AUTHOR

Margaret Feinberg is a beloved Bible teacher and speaker at churches and leading conferences. Her books, including *Wonderstruck, Fight Back With Joy, Taste and See,* and their corresponding Bible studies, have sold more than one million copies and received critical acclaim and extensive national media coverage from the Associated Press, *USA Today, The Washington Post*, and more.

She was named one of 50 women most shaping culture and the church today by *Christianity Today*. Margaret lives out West with her husband, Leif, and their superpup, Zoom. She believes some of the best days are spent in jammies, laughing, and being silly.

Let's be friends

www.margaretfeinberg.com

 Margaret Feinberg

 @mafeinberg

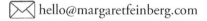 hello@margaretfeinberg.com

Stay Connected with Margaret

Visit MargaretFeinberg.com to:

- Receive free gifts and downloads
- Read Margaret's latest posts
- Watch a sneak peek of DVD Bible studies
- Save BIG when purchasing for your small group

DVD Bible Study Kits
from Margaret Feinberg

Fight Back With Joy will help you expand your joy threshold by awakening you to God's fierce love and escape fear and regret by applying biblical strategies to whatever crisis you're facing. Ranked one of the top 3 Bible studies of the year by Lifeway.

Scouting the Divine unlocks the deeper meaning of Scripture and takes you on a spiritual adventure. Margaret spent a year visiting shepherds, farmers, vintners, and beekeepers in order to better understand the agrarian themes in the Bible.

Wonderstruck: Awaken to the Nearness of God will help you renew your passion for God, discover peace in knowing you're wildy loved, and recognize the presence of God. Uncover how much God is busting at the seams to display His power, glory, and might in your life.

Available at MargaretFeinberg.com